The ArtScroll Series®

Rabbi Nosson Scherman / Rabbi Meir Zlotowitz
General Editors

RABBI YISROEL MILLER

Notes from the battlefield of human relationships

Mesorah Publications, ltd

WHAT'S WRONG WITH BEING HUMAN?

FIRST EDITION
First Impression . . . May 1992

Published and Distributed by
MESORAH PUBLICATIONS, Ltd.
Brooklyn, New York 11232

Distributed in Israel by
MESORAH MAFITZIM / J. GROSSMAN
Rechov Harav Uziel 117
Jerusalem, Israel

Distributed in Australia & New Zealand by
GOLD'S BOOK & GIFT CO.
36 William Street
Balaclava 3183, Vic., Australia

Distributed in Europe by
J. LEHMANN HEBREW BOOKSELLERS
20 Cambridge Terrace
Gateshead, Tyne and Wear
England NE8 1RP

Distributed in South Africa by
KOLLEL BOOKSHOP
22 Muller Street
Yeoville 2198, Johannesburg
South Africa

THE ARTSCROLL SERIES ®
WHAT'S WRONG WITH BEING HUMAN?
© Copyright 1992, by MESORAH PUBLICATIONS, Ltd.
4401 Second Avenue / Brooklyn, N.Y. 11232 / (718) 921-9000

No part of this book may be reproduced
in any form *without* **written** *permission from the copyright holder,*
except by a reviewer who wishes to quote brief passages in connection with a review
written for inclusion in magazines or newspapers.

THE RIGHTS OF THE COPYRIGHT HOLDER WILL BE STRICTLY ENFORCED.

ISBN:
0-89906-544-9 (hard cover)
0-89906-545-7 (paperback)

Printed in the United States of America by Noble Book Press Corp.
Bound by Sefercraft Quality Bookbinders, Ltd., Brooklyn, N.Y.

Table of Contents

Part I

Introduction	7
Strangers in Marriage	9
Parents and Prophets	25
The Importance of Being Old	40
In Search of Our Teacher Moshe	48
Something for Satan	63
The Secret of Being Wicked	73
Who Needs You?	87

Part II: Shorter Essays, Arranged by Sidrah

Lech Lecha: Standing Apart	99
Vayeira: The Joys of Social Pressure	104
Toldos: Yaakov and Eisav	109
Vayishlach: Divine Apologies	114
Vayechi: Cultural Bondage	118
Shemos: Passing On	122
Vaeira: Public Protests	125
Bo: Other People's Foolishness	129

Yisro: Parents and Adult Children	134
Terumah: Dishonest and Pious?	139
Vayikra: Having It All	144
Tazria: Unified Diversity	148
Metzora: The Dangers of Being Human	153
Kedoshim: Grudge-Bearing	157
Emor: Temporary Elevations	162
Bamidbar: Choosing a Team	166
Beha'aloscha: Teaching	171
Shelach: Idealistic Temptations	174
Korach: "It's the Principle of the Thing"	177
Matos: Gratitude	181
Ki Seitzei: Divine Messengers	186
Ki Savo: Mitzvah Blessings	190
Nitzavim: Covenant	194
Ha'azinu: Seventy Nations	198
Glossary	203

Introduction

> "... and the result is that one is truly placed in a difficult battle, for all the affairs of this world, whether good or bad, are trials ..." (Mesillas Yesharim).

These thirty-one essays are based on talks and *shiurim* given over the past ten years in Pittsburgh, Pennsylvania; Lakewood, New Jersey and several other communities. The ideas expressed include insights, practical tips and words of *chizuk* (encouragement) which thoughtful Jewish men and women of many different backgrounds have found beneficial, as a result of which many of the listeners have requested that the *shiurim* be published for them to review and to share.

> "... and the battle is upon him from all sides" (ibid.).

Nothing in these pages is intended to provide definitive answers to questions of Torah *hashkafah* (ideology) or practical halachah. The ideas are all only suggestions, notes from the battlefield to share with friends, including all the many friends I have not yet had the opportunity to meet.

> "The greater the difficulty ... the more they rejoice to show the strength of their loyalty, like a warrior famed for valor who chooses always the heaviest fighting" (ibid.).

These pages were written slowly, one paragraph at a time, and it is suggested that they be read the same way. After completing a chapter, it may be helpful to jot down a new idea or two, along with any practical application that comes to mind for everyday use.

A glossary of Hebrew words in the text is found at the back of the book. Words which are omitted are probably titles of *sefarim* (Torah books) or words whose meaning can be understood from the context in which they appear.

> *". . . and if he will be the warrior, and be victorious in the battle on all sides, it is he . . . who will merit to cleave to his Creator, to go out . . . to the light of life"* (*ibid*.).

Special thanks to all those who invited me to give the original *shiurim* upon which this book is based, including Rav Shaul Kagan of Pittsburgh's Kollel Beis Yitzchok: Rabbi Aaron Pam and Rabbi Yisroel Kellner of Beth Medrash Govoha's Summer Yarchei Kallah; and Alan Margolis, Elliot Falk, Lyon Mandelcorn and Rabbi Yisroel Pfeffer, presidents of Pittsburgh's Congregation Poale Zedeck, whom I have had the privilege of working with these past seven years.

Yasher koach to Avi Shulman and Mrs. Ruth Nayhouse, who prodded me to put the *shiurim* down in writing; to Mrs. Judi Dick of Mesorah Publications, whose skill and patience nursed the rough draft to completion; and to my daughters Nechama Liba and Yehudis, for their help and special insight.

Last but not least, I have no words with which to express proper gratitude to my wife Devora Glicka, whose support has been a source of courage for me on many a field of battle these nineteen years; and who, amidst all of life's ups and downs, has never lost faith that, with help from Hashem, ultimate victory awaits us all.

Yisroel Miller

Iyar, 5752

Strangers in Marriage

The year was 1972, and I was a young fellow learning in the *yeshivah* of Lakewood, New Jersey when a close friend married a girl from Brooklyn and entered the Lakewood Kollel. One can imagine the period of adjustment necessary for the bride, with her new husband, new home and new community to deal with all at once.

To make things easier, the *kallah* was welcomed and befriended by a next-door neighbor, a young woman only a couple of years older than herself. In one of their first conversations, the neighbor told the newlywed: "Yes, marriage is wonderful — for the first six months. After that, it is downhill, all the way."

As shocked as the bride was to hear this, its impact was worse for me, when my friend repeated it — because I was still a bachelor at the time. I found myself asking the age-old question: If indeed, this is the institution of marriage, do I really want to spend the rest of my life in an institution?

And I've been asking myself, ever since: Why must things be this way for so many marriages? When the wedding photographer says, "This is the happiest day of your life," is it inevitable that all subsequent days will be less happy? What causes the problems which seem to beset even the finest Torah families? Does the Torah give answers to solve the problems; and if so, where are these solutions to be found?

After all these years, I still do not have *the* answer. But I do have *an* answer, and I'd like to share it with you:

The reason why so many marriages fail is because failure is the most natural result of a wedding.

As our Sages told us, the Hebrew words for man and woman, אִישׁ, *ish*, and אִשָּׁה, *ishah,* both contain the word אֵשׁ, *eish,* fire. *Ish* and *ishah* also contain the letters י, *yud*, and ה, *hei*, of the Divine Name. And the Sages said: If the married couple lives with the *Shechinah,* the Divine Presence, then there is joy. If not, if the spark of Divinity is missing, then there only remains אֵשׁ, *eish*, twice, and one fire consumes the other.

This seems to say that, unless Hashem is an active force in your life and in your relationship, fire and explosion are the most natural course of events. That being the case, marriage counselors and women's magazines should not be asking why couples break up; but rather, how it is that some couples manage to stay together?

Available evidence seems to indicate that marital stability was much stronger in the good old days, even among non-Jews who did not live with the Divine Presence in their lives. One likely reason is that divorce was simply socially unacceptable, if not illegal. If you were stuck with a bad marriage, you put up with it, like a blister on your toe. Once you accepted the inevitable, it became easier to get along with and perhaps even to find happiness in the long run.

Another reason why things used to be better is that our Old World ancestors never heard of Thomas Jefferson, who wrote in the Declaration of Independence that everyone is endowed with an inalienable right to the "pursuit of happiness." Some years back, when American anthropologists asked native villagers in Turkey about their feelings on the pursuit of happiness, the villagers thought the anthropologists were *meshugah*. Pursue happiness? Happiness is a blessing granted by the Creator, and some are blessed and others not.

But today, if we don't feel happy, or if talk radio tells us it is time for a mid-life crisis, or if we take the Sunday newspaper's marital compatibility test and we don't like our score — then, goodbye marriage. Inalienable rights come first, don't they? As a philosopher once put it: The secret of being miserable is to have enough free time to ask yourself whether you are happy or not. In the old days they did not ask, and by and large were more content for it.

So, in today's throw-away society, it is not surprising that marriage faces so many difficulties, especially in light of *Chazal's* warning that the fires are always ready to consume one another from the start. But let me suggest that, instead of being cause for pessimism, this realization means that when we do face marital problems, we should know they are natural and normal, and not a sign that "*Oy*, I married the wrong one!" Take friction as a sign that, although he or she *is* the one, we must invest time and effort to build a relationship and to bring the *Shechinah,* the Divine Presence, into our lives.

I am not qualified to give advice on producing the *Shechinah.* But I can suggest two principles to help in the delicate work of creating a shared life, principles of practical value in everyday situations. The first principle is to know, beyond all doubt: I and my spouse are indeed united; whatever the difficulties may be, we are one, right now and forever. The second principle is to know: Although we are one, as close as two people can be, yet in some ways, each one remains a stranger to the other; in certain respects, I do not fully understand my spouse and never will.

Principle #1 is to know that the two of you are already one. The Gemara says that in *Eretz Yisrael* when a man married, they would ask (*Brachos* 8a): *"Matza, oh motzei?* Have you found her, or are you finding her?" This alluded to two references to women in *Tanach*: (a) *matza*, have you *found* her? as it says: *One who found a wife has found goodness* (*Proverbs* 18:22); (b) *motzei*, are you *finding* her? as it says: *I find the woman more bitter than death* (*Ecclesiastes* 7:26). This is a famous *gut vort,* a bon mot which has adorned many a *sheva brachos.* But what does it truly mean?

The difference between the two verses is that one is in the past tense, *found*, and the other is present, *finding*. Take a wooden board, six feet long and six inches wide, and place it on the floor. Could you walk its length without falling off? Certainly, with ease. Now take the same board and lift it thirty feet in the air. Could you still walk from one end to the other? It's not so easy. The wood is the same, but on the ground you *know* you can do it, and therefore you can. In the air, you begin to think: Maybe not? What if I slip and fall? And the uncertainty, the hesitation, creates a fear which causes us to tremble and possibly to lose our balance as well.

Matza ishah, one who has found a wife, has found goodness. Past tense: you found her, you are certain this *is* the one; then you are at peace. Because even when you hit the inevitable bumps in the road, there are no questions in your mind. You know, this person is mine, we are in it together, and together we will succeed. With that attitude, there is no doubt and no fear, and your natural sense of balance guides you along the way.

But *motzei*, finding, is present tense: One who says, "Well, we're getting to know each other's true selves. I'm discovering what she is really like. Maybe she is the right one for me. As the marriage progresses I'll find out." With that attitude of maybe yes, maybe no, there will be doubts and fears and endless second-guessing more bitter than death. Therefore in *Eretz Yisrael* they warned the young man — and today we can also counsel the young woman, or the older one — *matza*, know that once you say *mazel tov,* this is indeed the one; the one from Hashem, the name proclaimed in heaven forty days before you were born. You truly have found her, or him; and with that certainty, you will find goodness as well.

Principle #2 After you have finally recognized that you are indeed spiritually bound together, that it is this person with whom you can become one, you must then avoid the trap of believing that the two of you should therefore always think alike, share common interests — or even that you should fully understand each other.

The Torah teaches that Hashem created a mate for Adam because it is *not good for man to be alone* (*Genesis* 2:18). What is the meaning of *not good*? Does Adam need someone to go jogging with or to iron his shirts?

Rashi quotes the Midrash: If Adam is alone, one might think, there is one Hashem above and one Adam below, so Adam is also a god! But this is difficult to understand, because it appears that the Creator had always intended to create additional people, Adam's offspring, with or without Eve. If there would be no women or marriage and the whole world would consist of four billion bachelors, how could each of them think, "I am the only one, I am a deity?"

The meaning is: Without marriage, I am intellectually aware that other people exist. But on the emotional level, inside, where one really lives, I am the only one in the world. I choose friends who make me happy and activities that please me. The only desire which is important, the only will which occupies my mind twenty-four hours a day is my own. Inside myself, *I* become the god, and the rest of the world exists only to do my bidding.

That may sound exaggerated. But how often do I find myself

Strangers in Marriage

waiting in a supermarket checkout line, and fuming: "What's taking so long?" That really means: "How dare they do their shopping when *I*, the lord of the universe, want to go through?" Some people will curse at heavy traffic, get angry at an unexpected snowstorm or become infuriated when their car fails to start. The true meaning of that anger is: "How dare Hashem make a world in which reality is not the way *I* want it to be?"

If we cannot force others to worship us on the outside, we often try to do so at home. After all, what other purpose do my parents have in life but to make me happy? And how do those children in *shul* have the *chutzpah* to behave like — children? And how selfish my neighbors are, always acting in their own best interest; why can't they be like me and act in *my* best interest? Thus, a human being, created in the image of Hashem, withers away and degenerates into a little ball of miserable complaints, whining that the world will not devote itself to making him happy.

It is not good for Adam to be alone. It will ruin him, or her. Therefore the Creator fashioned *eizer kenegdo,* a helper opposing him, different from him; different ways of thinking and feeling and acting, which force him to confront the existence of an "other." He must focus on another life, another will, and must take that will into consideration; he is forced out of the prison of self-absorption, to learn to adjust to the needs of another human being.

The *navi* said: *It is good for a young man to bear a yoke* (*Eichah* 3:27). What is this yoke which is good? What sort of burden ultimately brings gladness and joy? The Midrash answers: This refers to the yoke of marriage. There truly *is* a burden, one *must* learn to adjust; but that is only because it is a necessary step to develop, leading on to joy.

Mesichta Derech Eretz Zuta tells us: To develop love for another person, make yourself busy doing kindnesses for *him* or *her*. A mother does so much for her child, yet it causes the mother to love the child more than the child loves the mother. The marriage burden, the yoke of having to understand another person and make allowances for their feelings and special needs — that is what creates the love and the joy of what marriage was meant to be.

To take a practical example, there is a *mitzvah* of *simchas Yom Tov*, rejoicing on festivals. How should we rejoice? A man opens his Gemara and reads: *Simchah* is (brought about) with wine. He runs to his local kosher wine shop for a bottle of their best, and then he thinks: Perhaps I should buy two bottles, one for myself and one for my wife? But the Gemara says: No. Just because wine gives you *simchah*, it doesn't mean it will give her *simchah*. Consider her needs; buy her a new dress for *Yom Tov*.

The husband is flabbergasted. An eight-dollar bottle of wine for him, and a one hundred and eighty-dollar dress for her? Is the expression of *simchah*, of spiritual joy for him, not good enough for her? But that revelation is exactly the point: that two people, as close as two human beings can be, nevertheless retain individual identities, with different feelings and different joys; and each one must recognize and respect the differences which exist. This perception allows me to appreciate that my spouse is indeed a person, and that I have been blessed with another soul with whom to share my life; and I am not alone.

If this is true in *mitzvos*, it is certainly true in personal desires. One woman complained that her husband did not share her cultural or recreational interests, and I told her: Your only legitimate complaint might be that perhaps you husband should learn to become a better actor, to be able to at least *pretend* that he enjoys what you do. But to actually expect a spouse to share all the same joys — that is a mistaken perception of what marriage is in the first place.

If I may be forgiven a personal reference: I encourage my own wife to buy clothing for herself, and within the limits of our budget, I am pleased when she does so. But she is a person who lives simply and does not desire an expensive wardrobe. Instead, all *she* wants is to be able to telephone her mother regularly — and her mother lives in Great Britain. I am happy to give her what *I* want to give; but Rav Yisrael Salanter said:

Chesed, kindness to others, is when you give them what *they* want to receive.

These differences show themselves everywhere, sometimes even in areas of *halachah* where we would expect perfect uniformity. The Gemara states that one is obligated to recline at the Pesach *Seder*, and most *Rishonim* (medieval commentators) rule that this obligation applies today to both men and women. A minority opinion, the *Raviah*, rules that in our times the obligation to recline is no longer in effect for men *or* women. The final *halachah* is: Men follow the opinion that we must recline. Women follow the opinion that it is no longer necessary.

It is a novel idea to note that in some areas women have their own *minhag*, a halachic practice different from that of men. Our Sages tell us "women are a separate nation," a different culture. Just as Americans and Europeans cannot easily comprehend the workings of a Japanese mind, all the more so should you not expect to easily comprehend the thoughts of your own spouse.

It has been said that the love between husband and wife is to provide a *mashal*, an analogy, to the love between Hashem and the Jewish people. We could suggest that just as we can love Hashem without ever understanding His essence, love between husband and wife can in the same way be complete and eternal, without ever fully understanding what it is that makes the other person tick. A desire to know someone completely sometimes stems from a desire to control them. It is not necessary nor is it necessarily healthy.

To sum up: We have offered an approach to Torah marriage, which is (1) to know with certainty that this person with whom I share my life is the *right* person, given to me by Heaven; and (2) at the same time, to know that I can never know this person completely; he or she remains an "other" whom I must work to understand, and the work is a task which will never be completed.

In a true Torah marriage, when husbands and wives do live with these ideals, how do they put them into practice? Where

does it affect their behavior? There are at least four distinct areas:
>   1) Increased sensitivity.
>   2) Acceptance of alternative views of reality.
>   3) Learning to respond to emotions.
>   4) Demonstrating gratitude.

1) Increased Sensitivity

Most married couples treat one another with a lack of courtesy they would never dream of showing strangers. One reason for this is the feeling that we need not be quite so formal, which is certainly true. But very often we hurt those we love with callous inattention or an off-the-cuff insult because we think: "It's OK"; "She understands"; "He doesn't mind"; "She's not so sensitive; and if she is, it's her own fault." Once we realize that we do not truly understand the other person, that we have no real idea what goes on in that person's mind, we will come to ask ourselves the terrifying question: "What horrible things have I done to wound the very person I love? What enduring scars have I created unknowingly, and what can I possibly do to make amends?"

Am I overstating the case? Do you think that most spouses are not touchy, not so sensitive? The Torah tells us: When our mother Sarah heard she would be blessed with a child in her old age, she laughed and said: "After I have become withered, will I have a child? And my husband is old." Hashem then told Avraham: "Why did Sarah laugh, saying, 'How can I have a child now that I am old?' "

The Gemara points out that Hashem misquoted Sarah. She had said that she was withered, and her husband was old. Hashem repeated it as: *She* is old, and He omitted the reference to her husband. Why did Hashem not quote her precisely? The Gemara answers, to keep peace in the family. Had our father Avraham heard that our mother Sarah said *he* was old, his feelings could have been hurt!

Can you imagine that? Avraham Avinu, the giant of *tzaddikim*, close to one hundred years old, will feel hurt if his wife says (to herself!) that her husband is old? It was the truth. Both of them were senior citizens, and Sarah did not view it as an insult. The Torah is teaching us: As far as *we* are concerned, we must always assume the other person is super-sensitive. You think that your spouse doesn't care? Perhaps. But be careful anyway, because even if you're married to our father Avraham, you should never take anything for granted.

As a teen-ager, I spent one summer in camp teaching Torah to a group of nine-year-old boys. Controlling the class was not easy (more my fault than theirs), and I bore down hard on one particularly irritating troublemaker. Fifteen years later I discovered that this boy's father, a respected community figure, was an alcoholic. To this day, I ask myself: How did I not have the sensitivity to feel this child's inner pain? Perhaps the trick is to realize that *everyone* we meet, even those we think we know, suffers from some inner pain; and we must treat them gently, because we don't know where it hurts.

2) Acceptance of Alternative Views of Reality

A second area where it helps to understand that we *don't* understand is to accept that in our spouse's mind there exists a very different picture of reality. Each of us is raised a different way, and we grow up thinking that our way is not only better, but normal, and other ways are not. For example: American restaurants serve bacon, while restaurants in Korea serve dog meat. I have never tasted either of those items; but for some odd reason, I think of bacon as a normal food for humans, while dog meat is not. There is no real difference; but my culture, the environment in which I was raised, gave me a mental picture of reality and normality which may be untrue, but which adheres.

That particular example will not cause any problems, except for an American gentile who marries a Korean. But consider the simple matter of time. A Pittsburgh wedding invitation announced a *chupah* for 7 p.m. and it began at 7:20, which is normal in that city. A guest from Brooklyn arrived at 7:40, missed the *chupah* and instead of apologizing, exploded in anger: "How could you make the *chupah* so early without telling us in advance?" Even if they are from the same community, husband and wife may come from families with very different views on what it means to be on time, and much minor irritation can be avoided by recognizing that the same words often mean very different things to different people.

There are hundreds of other examples. Loud speech is irritating, but families have different ideas of how loud is Loud. People from out west often speak more slowly than New Yorkers do. Does the New Yorker talk too fast or the westerner too slowly? Even as regards the question of distance, how close to stand while conversing, some people think that Mexicans are "pushy" because they come right up to you; but many Mexicans think that Americans are cold because they stand so far away. Both views are equally "normal" and we must realize that each individual, including the person we marry, has at the very least, a slightly different view of this world. It is worth spending time to discover as best you can what that view is, if you hope to share a home and a heart.

3) Learning to Respond to Emotions

A third area where it helps to know that married couples do not fully comprehend one another is in learning to respond to emotions, a category which includes many problems. A common example is anger. A man has a hard day at work and he comes home and criticizes his wife's cooking. She reacts with anger of her own or else feels guilty that she's not a good cook. Either way, she is missing the point. The Gemara says: Anger is an internal false god. Even without knowing the full profundity of this Gemara, it is teaching us that her act did not *cause* his anger. It only triggered the devil that was already eating away at him internally, feelings of failure or guilt or whatever creates the inner pain.

To take an extreme case, if someone expresses a hatred for those who learn Torah — "I would like to bite him!" — is that a sign of extreme wickedness? Or does it perhaps indicate a potential Rabbi Akiva, who felt that degree of hatred before he started learning, in his burning envy for the Torah he desired but had never pursued?

When we know that we do not know the other person's mind, we no longer need to respond to anger by defending ourselves or by counter-attacking. We accept that he or she is hurting for reasons unknown, we do not automatically blame ourselves and we see what we can do to soothe the pain. Sometimes it is enough just to show a little sympathy: "You must have had a terrible day; I feel for you."

Since we cannot read another person's mind, then surely we must accept that they cannot read ours. A wife asks her husband, "Shall I make you a cup of coffee?" He says, "No, don't trouble yourself." Does that mean NO? Or does it mean: "Don't trouble yourself unless you care about me, in which case you would make it without me even asking?"

Do not hate your brother in secret (*Leviticus* 19:17). Let him, or her, know what's bothering you. This does not mean we should go around telling everybody exactly what we think of them. But it does mean: If it bothers you that the dishes are not done, let her know. Even better, grab a dishtowel and help. Accept that the other person may be super-sensitive; that he has a different picture of what is normal; that we must be careful in responding to emotions and in verbalizing our own.

4) Demonstrating Gratitude

It is all important to express gratitude. We are taught as children to say please and thank you, and *yeshivos* teach about *hakaras hatov,* that gratitude is an integral part of Torah. But we often fail to see that in marriage, gratitude is more than just important. It is absolutely vital.

The *Ramban* writes that Adam was first created without a wife so that he would feel lonely and appreciate Eve when she appeared. But if so, then shouldn't Adam have been created without hands or feet, without hearing or speech, so that he would also feel their absence and appreciate those blessings from Hashem when they were bestowed? Since only Eve was delayed, it seems that the Torah is teaching us: Although one should be grateful for all blessings, the greatest of all is a wife, and though he may take his other blessings for granted, he dare not be indifferent to the gift of his personal Eve.

Many husbands and wives say that they *do* appreciate their spouses, but they don't have to keep on expressing it. "She knows I appreciate her." "He knows I'm grateful for what he does." But if you accept the profound truth that you truly do *not* know what he or she really thinks, that we cannot take anything for granted; then surely we may never take kindness for granted, but we must always express our thanks, in an infinite number of ways.

To return to the analogy of our relationship with Hashem: Even though a perfect *tzaddik* feels true gratitude to Hashem for every blessing he receives, still, his *feelings* are not enough. He is nonetheless obligated to express his gratitude with a *brachah*, a blessing, a hundred blessings each day. We can also learn from this analogy that if we don't fully feel the emotion of gratitude, we say the *brachah* anyway; and therefore, whether you feel it or not, a thank-you is surely appropriate for kindness received from other people as well.

Rabbi Avigdor Miller wrote that the word *hallel*, a *song of praise*, is related to *holelus*, wildness. The word *shevach* also means praise, but *hallel* is "to go wild about something," to get carried away with emotion. The word *hallel* is used to praise Hashem, but not only Hashem. In *Eishes Chayil,* describing the Woman of Valor: *Her children praise her* (*Mishlei* 31:28), but her husband: *yehalelah,* her husband goes *wild* about her. That's the way to be; and if your wife is not yet the perfect *eishes chayil,* maybe that is the way to encourage her to become one. Or maybe her flaws are a reflection of your own.

Of course, it works both ways and she must also express her gratitude towards him. But all those wonderful words which we hear only at a *hesped*, eulogizing someone who has departed — please, don't wait till then. He or she doesn't really know how you feel, unless you say it. And even if you said it yesterday, and the day before and the day before — fifty years of reciting *Birchas Hamazon* does not absolve you from saying it yet again today. The same is true of all sincere thanks and honest compliments; he or she will never tire of listening.

We have suggested a general approach: Accept your spouse as Heaven-sent for you, and at the same time he/she is so Heavenly that you cannot fully understand him/her. We also explored four areas where this attitude will make a difference: Considering the likelihood that he or she is hypersensitive; recognizing that they view reality differently; being careful how we respond to emotions or how we express our own, and remembering to demonstrate gratitude every opportunity we have.

To bring these lessons home, let's look at a common marital situation in which the above principles all come into play, and that is: when your beloved spouse does something which drives you up a wall. Whether it is a relatively minor problem like poor table manners or a major calamity like behavior that threatens to destroy the family, Heaven forbid, certain principles in dealing with a spouse apply to almost every situation.

First, we must know that we cannot expect to change another person's fundamental personality and basic character traits. Rav Yisrael Salanter taught that it is easier to learn *Shas*, the entire Talmud, than to change one character trait. Ninety-nine percent of us have never done it, so we should not expect to see that transformation in someone else.

Instead, our only reasonable goal must be a change in *behavior*, what Rav Yisrael Salanter called *kevishas hamiddos;* the character trait remains, but steps are taken that it should not manifest itself in daily activity. An alcoholic cannot be cured of his desire to drink, but with help and constant reinforcement he can learn to abstain from the *act* of drinking. A husband who is stingy with money, or who does not understand the need to spend time with his wife, may never change his nature. But it is possible to modify his behavior, which usually is all that is really necessary.

Bear in mind the four points made above: Assume that others are super-sensitive about criticism. Assume they have a different view of reality, and they do not share your point-of-view even after you explain it (if they were so "rational," they would not be doing this sort of thing to begin with). Assume that any conversation in which the emotions take over makes communication impossible, because we cannot read minds and we will misinterpret the message. And finally, remember: Other people need continual emotional support, to feel needed and appreciated, even when you are criticizing them.

If you attack, saying: "Your sloppiness is disgusting!" or if you make a moral issue out of it: "You don't care about me!" or, worst of all, if you make it into an issue of loyalty to Torah: "That is not the way a Jewish wife or husband is supposed to act!" — that kind of talk violates *all* the principles mentioned above. The other people are deeply hurt; they want to defend themselves, or attack you in return; they hear nothing of what you say; and they wonder, why did they ever marry such a terrible person who doesn't love or appreciate them?

What can you say? *Rav Yosef Leib Bloch of Telz* pointed out that if we demand *kavod*, if we tell someone that they owe us honor and respect; then his natural reaction is to say, "No, prove it to me!" However, if it is not a demand, not expressed as a moral obligation, if, instead, we make others aware of our own personal need, then most people are magnanimous enough to want to help.

That means: Instead of the word "you" — *you* are wrong, *you* should change, etc. — we should use the word "I." "I love you. I appreciate all the wonderful things you do and are. But, when I have to pick up your shirt from the floor, every day, it bothers me, and I find that I just can't take it anymore."

Even in a most serious situation, such as physical abuse, the general approach is: "I love you, and I want very much to be with you, but I cannot live this way. If it continues, I have no choice but to leave or to call the police. Please help me; let's work together so that does not happen." (Certainly, expert guidance may be needed in serious cases.) No solutions are guaranteed. But this approach at least encourages the other person to listen, instead of increasing his resentment.

One final tip: *The words of the wise are heeded to when they are spoken gently* (*Ecclesiastes* 9:17). Speaking softly keeps the anger from surfacing and allows you to get your message across without interference from emotional static.

In our house, when a child screams for something, we sometimes say: "Don't yell. Talk nicely." One winter I came down with a mild case of laryngitis and I was whispering. My three-year-old daughter looked up at me in surprise, and she asked: "Tatty, why are *you* talking nicely?"

That is a lesson to remember, a lesson for parents and children, husbands and wives, and every human being.

It takes time and effort to achieve great things, but the reward is worth it. Since marriage is a *mitzvah* of the Torah, and the Gemara says that the *Shechinah*, the Divine Presence, is a necessary component of marriage; it must be that the *Shechinah*, living with Hashem in your own home, is possible for everyone. And surely, in addition to all the other practical advice, we must also *daven*, pray for peace and harmony, and ask, as we do in *Maariv*:

"Hashem, guide us with good advice, Your advice; to give us life and peace, from now on till forever, in this world and the World to Come" (*the daily Evening Service*).

Parents and Prophets

In the next chapter ("The Importance of Being Old"), we explain the principle that in any *mitzvah* which requires us to give something to another person, the ultimate purpose of the *mitzvah* is not to benefit that person, but to benefit ourselves. Giving *tzedakah* to the needy elevates the donor and honoring a parent improves the soul of the child.

In the same way, the *mitzvos* of child-rearing, of *chinuch* or education, should not be viewed as having been given because "somebody had to do it." The Creator could have endowed babies with sufficient maturity to care for themselves, just as fish and many animals do. But the *mitzvah* of *chinuch* was given to us because in raising a child, we end up raising ourselves.

Parenting changes us, in most cases, for the good, and in important ways. It compels us to mature and to accept responsibilities; it forces us to clarify our own values and goals; and it pushes us to empathize, to try to comprehend the feelings of a little creature who is so very different from ourselves. When the Haggadah says that the Torah tells us to respond differently to each of four sons, it means that each child brings out *kochos hanefesh,* a different depth in our personality as we struggle to respond to each one in his or her own individual way.

So perhaps the introduction to true Torah parenting is to realize that the *mitzvah* is for *my* own benefit. While in the midst of the work, and all the pain — pain there certainly is, the Sages call it *tza'ar gidul banim*, or the pain of raising children — in my efforts to make my child into a *mentch*, I should remember: This is all part of Hashem's plan to help make a *mentch* out of me.

What kind of *mentch*? What image is a Jewish mother or father supposed to convey? *Sefer HaChinuch* writes: Parents are meant to be a *mashal*, an analogy. Through observation of the father and mother who gave life to me, I am to recognize the Creator Who gave life to us all. Parents are a *mashal* to Hashem, which explains why the Torah compares the reverence to be given my father and mother with my obligation of reverence to my Father in Heaven.

This analogy is more than a theoretical ideal. King Shlomo said: "The words of King Lemuel, the prophecy with which his mother rebuked him" (*Mishlei* 31:1). What was the prophecy? The commentary of *Metzudas David* explains: "The words of rebuke from his mother were to him like a prophecy of the Word of Hashem."

The goal of parenting is that even when grown, the individual continues to hear the voice of his parents as the voice of Hashem's prophets. *Rav Chaim Shmulevitz z.l.* added: Part of the *mitzvah* of honoring parents is to see them as *gedolei hador,* to view them as possessors of spiritual greatness.

I don't know about you, but to me these ideas can be pretty depressing. It's hard enough to get up in the morning without having to ask myself if the face in the mirror looks like a prophet, or if my five-year-old listens to my words like the *Devar Hashem.* But the purpose of this is not to depress anyone. To the contrary, it is to remind us that parenting is the noblest of professions; to remind us that if, for example, a mother does not work outside the home, she has every right to be proud of her demanding career; and to remind us that Torah parenting is a job for men as well, and it is an honor for anyone to be able to serve as a prophetic role model for a future servant of Hashem.

Let us bring these lofty concepts down to a level for all of us and offer some suggestions we can use day-to-day.

The Gemara says that the Sages would often ask the son of a great man, "In what *mitzvah* was your father outstanding?" Those spiritual giants were outstanding in every *mitzvah*; but in addition, each *tzaddik* chose one special *mitzvah* as his own, fulfilling its every aspect without exception; one *mitzvah* in which to shine and which his children recognized and remembered. *Rav Moshe Shternbuch* wrote that this is a custom of *tzaddikim* even in our time. You may not be the Chofetz Chaim, but each parent can be perceived by his or her child as someone special, if one adopts some special *mitzvah* or some area of Torah practice that is uniquely his or hers.

For many of us, excelling in even one *mitzvah* may prove difficult. But it does not have to be an entire *mitzvah*; even one aspect can suffice. *Yesod VeShoresh HaAvodah* wrote that just as there are *chiddushei Torah,* novel Torah insights, so too are there *chiddushei Avodah,* novel ways in which all of us, men and women, can honor Hashem. This does not refer to new extra-strict *chumros* (stringencies) nor does it require eccentric behavior.

I cannot recall the *divrei Torah* or even the conversations which took place at our Shabbos table when I was a child, but I will never forget our Shabbos *Kiddush*, when my mother a.h. would insist that all the children stand quietly with their hands behind their backs. It was a symbol of honor, a *kavod Shabbos* which was special because it was our family tradition; and it is a tradition I pass on to my own children today. This was ours, just as we had our special family *zemiros*, and stories and recipes for Shabbos and Succos and Pesach, sanctified to us by their hallowed repetition year after year after year.

Family tradition — even if not worthy of the name *minhag*, whatever particular customs and rituals make up your *mishpachah's* service to Hashem — is a legacy which is remembered and perpetuated, and which helps to make our parents special Jews.

So consider: What are the special practices, the *mitzvah* routines and singular rituals in your family? What new ones should you deliberately create (after consulting your Rav, naturally) for your children to see? And which old ones should you strengthen, to give them a permanent place of honor? Let the children recognize that this *mishpachah* is made up of a unique combination of spiritual flavors; and if the parent is not a "big *gadol*" (great Torah giant), at least let him or her be seen as "a little *gadol*," the creator of an individual Torah contribution to the world, a creation of which the child partakes and has a share in its perpetuation.

It is important for your son or daughter to see you as someone special, for their sake; they need you to be that *navi*, that prophetic *mashal* to inspire them. You can often make it easier, by enlisting the aid of another member of the family. For instance, in our family, we are very proud of the fact that my father *shlita* was a congregational rabbi for over thirty years and in all that time remained a scrupulously honest man. (If you don't think that is an accomplishment, you are probably not an American pulpit rabbi.)

But at some point in my adulthood I asked myself, how do I know my father was outstandingly honest? I never checked his tax returns (the fact that we never had much money is not positive proof). And yet that belief is in my bones, because I heard it from my mother *a.h.* so many times. She would speak of my father's honesty and unique integrity in passing, as something *pashut*, a self-evident truth; and we children absorbed it as such, to inspire us as an ideal even today.

You may not be very convincing in trying to persuade your children to see you as a prophet. But you can let them know, again and again, that your spouse is truly outstanding, in one virtue or another.

Preferably, find something complimentary to say which is also true. If you really can't think of anything, then at least mention how good your spouse is to you and for you (it's true, you know). That's a lesson the child will hear and learn and apply to his own spouse someday. In a single-parent family, that is the function uncles and aunts can serve, to tell the child how much they themselves admire the child's parent, an admiration the child will absorb and imitate as years go by.

As a prophet in training, you will want to try to learn to speak like a *chacham*, one possessed of wisdom. This includes: *The words of the wise are heeded to when they are spoken gently* (*Ecclesiastes* 9:17). (See the chapter on marriage for a story on this principle.) Try going through an entire breakfast with your children in which you at no time raise your voice. You might enjoy the experience so much that you will give it a shot at lunch and dinner too.

The Gemara mentions yet another method to make children respect your words like words of prophecy: "If a person has fear of Heaven, people listen to him." That is surely a special blessing, a gift from Heaven. But also on a more simple level, people listen to the *yorei Shamayim* (God-fearing individual) because they know that he does not venture to speak unless he has something important to say.

How often do we think before we speak, especially in talking with children? To consider what to say, how to say it, and whether or not to say it at all? A biographer of Leo Tolstoy followed him around, recording his conversation to be included in a book. You can bet that being shadowed vastly improved the quality of Tolstoy's table talk; it kept him on his toes. Since in Heaven they record every word of all of us, we can also pause to arrange a thought, to speak for posterity, and to let the child recognize that what the old folks say is worth listening to, at least sometimes.

One more point about being a *navi*: "A prophet could not receive the Divine Presence, he could not function as a *navi*, unless he was filled with *simchah*." To give over something positive to a child, you must be in a positive mood to begin with. And how can the child feel good about Torah, if his parental role-model doesn't even feel good about himself?

Ultimately, we all need a strong dose of *bitachon*, to live with the joyous serenity of knowing that Hashem is indeed taking care. However, even for those individuals who have not yet attained such faith, some good advice is: You cannot work on developing *simchah* if you are not getting adequate sleep.

In the great *yeshivah* of Rav Simcha Zissel Ziv there was a *seder*, a special time, set aside for taking walks. *Rambam* writes that you cannot achieve spiritual progress if you do not feel well.

An *eishes chayil* who blames herself for losing her temper, or for insufficient trust in Hashem, may discover that what she really needs is a babysitter, a good nap and a chance to take a walk with her husband; and it can be a great *mitzvah* to encourage her to do so.

However, if she took the nap, went out for the walk and returned to find her house looking like a bomb hit it, and the kids have managed to cover everything with peanut butter except for the baby (who is covered with jelly), how could she keep from exploding? How did Lemuel's mother remain the prophetess when her child was acting up, with all the daily aggravation — *tza'ar gidul banim* — which is an integral part of parenting? Let me offer two practical tips, either of which can be a lifesaver.

Practical Tip #1. To be the *navi*, and the link to Hashem, you have to know and accept that aggravation is a *nisayon*, a challenge, whose chief purpose is to elevate you to a higher level of greatness. One reason Moshe Rabbeinu was chosen by Hashem was that a little sheep once spent an afternoon running him ragged; and when he finally caught up with it, instead of venting his frustration, he said, "You must be tired," and he carried the sheep back to the flock on his shoulder. Hashem said: Moshe, you can take care of the lambs, you are the one to be a leader in *Klal Yisrael.*

To apply this principle: Can you imagine giving a public lecture while every single member of the audience is trying to disturb you? A friend of mine did just that, and it was not terribly difficult. He was a student in a Torah Umesorah public-speaking course. Part of the training was an exercise in which each student took a turn to deliver a speech, while his audience — all the other students — tried their very best to annoy him. Picture yourself speaking to twenty senior *yeshivah* students and *kollel* scholars, while one of them is throwing spitballs, another incessantly clicks his pen, a third is coughing and so forth.

Horrible! But it wasn't, not really. Because he knew it was only a test, it was not quite real. If this is the game, there is no reason for you to be shaken by it, and you can enjoy the challenge and succeed. So when you find yourself faced with screaming toddlers, sulking teenagers or ten-year-old experts in psychological warfare, remember: Hashem is sitting there grading your report card, hoping you will recognize it is all only a test; you can keep your cool and be *zocheh* to the greatness that you were indeed meant to achieve.

Practical Tip #2: To handle petty aggravation, keep in mind that there is a Divine process called *kapparah*, atonement for sin. Almost everybody has at least a couple of sins to his account, and the Gemara tells us that virtually any kind of suffering atones for the sin and cleanses the soul. We do not usually pray for such *kapparah*, we don't ask to suffer. However, since a certain amount is inevitable, why not grab a pencil and paper, make a private list of sins you've committed in the last year or two (use both sides of the paper if necessary), and then ask yourself: "What would be a fair number of *tzaros*, personal aggravations, to make up for all the aggravations I have caused my Father in Heaven by my sins?"

Perhaps you are one of those rare saintly people who have no sins at all? If so, the *sefarim* tell us that *tzaddikim* like you are happy to accept *yisurim* to help atone for the rest of us! So either way, consider: What is a reasonable amount of suffering for this week?

I don't know about you. But for myself, I think that if my nine-year-old would spill a glass of milk or two, and if *chas veshalom* my three-year-old would crayon on the wallpaper, again; and even if *chalilah* I would find that the baby has been using the tape recorder as a toy in the bathtub — even so, between me and my Creator, I think I'm getting a bargain.

According to the *Chofetz Chaim*, writing in a slightly different context, the trick is to decide in advance that it is worth losing a certain amount; and then when it occurs, you are already mentally prepared to chalk it up to your account. If I expect at least one temper tantrum at breakfast, then when it happens I don't have to be upset by it. Once we get used to the idea of accepting what the *Ribono Shel Olam* sends us, then we can also get used to the idea that it is indeed He Who is doing the sending, that He is in complete charge and we can relax and enjoy all His blessings as well.

(This of course is not to imply that we should accept all harassment without responding to it. Just as we accept illness as Heaven sent while we seek medical treatment at the same time, so too can we accept petty aggravations with equanimity while we strive to prevent their recurrence.)

If all the above advice still doesn't work; if you are just so furious that you are ready to wring your beloved sweetheart's neck, then you should keep the following quotation posted on your refrigerator (I heard it said in the name of the *Chasam Sofer*): "Sometimes, my children are not nearly as good as I was when I was their age. But I guess that just goes to show that *my* father was better than theirs."

To sum up, we have suggested that since *mitzvos* involving others are given to us for our own benefit, the *mitzvah* of parenting is therefore meant to develop the parent, to make the parent into a spiritual *mashal* and a surrogate prophet. We have considered practical tips like creating personalized *mitzvos* and family traditions; building up your spouse in the eyes of the children; practicing volume control to speak gently and with forethought; and striving to become a role-model of *simchah*, learning to relax, to view aggravation as a test and to recognize in advance the need for a certain number of petty problems, budgeting for them and accepting their presence with gracious equanimity.

Let's take these lessons one step further. The Book of Samuel tells us there are two names for a prophet, *navi* and *ro'eh* (*I Samuel* 9:9). What do they mean? *Ro'eh* is the one who *sees*, who is granted a vision, knowledge from Hashem. *Navi* means the one who *speaks*, who communicates that vision to others. The *ro'eh* is an elevated individual, a role-model of sanctity for others to emulate. But it is not always enough for the *ro'eh* to just sit back and wait for others to follow. He or she must also become the *navi*, the one who transmits the message and actively guides others, whether they request it or not.

The same is true in parenting. We are to be the *ro'eh*, the model and *mashal* in all that we are and do. But in addition, one must also work to become a *navi*, to develop the skill to transmit the message, to effectively communicate the lessons to our children in a way they will accept.

How does one communicate? When Moshe Rabbeinu requested a successor, he asked Hashem to appoint a leader with *ruach*, "spirit." What is *ruach*? *Targum Unkelos* says it is *ruach nevuah*, prophecy, the spirit of a *navi*. Rashi writes that *ruach* is the ability to deal with each individual person, to understand where he is coming from and to respond to each one on his or her individual level.

At first glance it appears that *Rashi* differs with the *Targum* which translated *ruach* as *nevuah*. But by applying what we have said before, *Rashi* and the *Targum* are closely linked: A *navi* is one who can give over the Divine message; but part of the method of accomplishing this is to learn to understand each person as an individual, to place yourself on his plane of thought and understanding, to empathize and to relate to him in a way he can comprehend.

That is why *Koheles* emphasizes that King Shlomo, the wisest of all men, created parables, allegorical stories, enlightening illustrations; because wisdom is useless unless it is presented in a manner capable of being absorbed by those who are not yet wise.

To apply that lesson on our own level: We know that *mitzvos* are classified as either *mishpatim*, commandments which make sense to the human mind (e.g. honesty or charity); or *chukim*, commandments whose reasons are unclear to us (e.g. prohibitions against *sha'atnez* and non-kosher foods). Part of parental wisdom is in realizing that to children, especially younger children, virtually *everything* one says is *chukim*, mystical decrees whose reasons are unknown. Tell a three-year-old to please remove his fingers from the milk container or to refrain from wiping his hands on the wallpaper, and he may obey you. But do not expect him to understand the logic of your command and certainly you should not become angry that he does not understand it. Our toddler once uttered a bad word she had overheard somewhere, and when we told her not to say it, she obeyed. But for the next half-hour she went around innocently exclaiming: "I'm not supposed to say . . . (the word), I'm not supposed to say . . . ."

Even with older children, it is an article of faith that every other kid has a later bedtime, better toys and fewer household chores. Logic has nothing to do with this. One opinion in the Gemara (as explained by *Rashi*) says that children do not attain *da'as*, full moral comprehension, until age sixteen. Another opinion says: Eighteen! Teaching should begin at birth. But we must never forget: Children are beings from a different planet and it takes a long time before they learn the meaning of all the *chukim* we try to teach.

All this is part of the famous verse, *Train the child according to his way* (*Proverbs* 22:6). *His way* obviously means the way of a child, to keep in mind that children are very different from adults. The *pasuk* also has a second meaning: *Train the child according to his way*, i.e. according to his particular *individual* way, because every single child is different from every other. Even if you have read Dr. Spock, Dr. Ginot, and the pediatric authority who is "in" this year and even if you have already raised twenty-three wonderful children, it is all no guarantee for the twenty-fourth, because each human being is a complex universe, unique in creation.

This is very much tied into our theme of becoming a "surrogate prophet"; the *Vilna Gaon* explained that each person must guard his *mitzvos* in the way which is most suited to his personal nature, even if his path sometimes appears improper to others who do not understand his nature. He also said that even someone with a bad nature should not try to oppose it completely, because he cannot succeed. Instead, he must train himself to do what is right, while working in accordance with the needs of his particular personality.

For example, he said: Some people are born in the *mazal* of bloodletting and they are destined to shed blood. But they still possess free will to choose to do this in a permitted manner, such as becoming a *shochet* or even a *mohel*, rather than a criminal. This is the meaning of *Train the child according to his way*.

The *Gaon* explained that this was a major function of a *navi*: to peer into the soul of the Jew who came to him and to show that Jew what must be his or her individual *derech*, his or her special way to make maximum progress in Torah and *mitzvos* (*Even Shleimah*).

We have no *navi* today to peer into our souls. But the *Cheshbon HaNefesh* writes: Every parent is obligated to study his child to determine what are his or her special *middos*, their traits of character; in order to help the child to see himself accurately, to be able to grow as an adult.

You may think you already know your child, but consider

the following: *Sefarim* tell us that each person has one *middah*, one character trait, in which he possesses *gadlus*, (at least potential) greatness. Maximum success comes by building one's *Yiddishkeit* on the foundation of that *middah*. If you were asked, would you be able to say what is that one *middah*, in each of your children? For that matter, could you say what the one *middah* is in your spouse or even in yourself? It is a time-consuming study, and most people are not even aware that the subject exists.

Further analysis: *Sefarim* make a distinction between *middos*, traits of character, which can be changed for the better, and *kochos hanefesh*, traits of fundamental personality, which cannot be changed but must be sublimated and directed towards good. If you would make a list of your child's shortcomings (or of your own), could you tell which fault should be corrected, and which should be accepted and worked with? Most parents could not, because most of us have never bothered to make the list, neither the faults nor the strengths, and we lose because of it.

Part of knowing a child is to perceive the spirituality in a child's individual interests or special talents. *Rav Yosef Chaim of Bagdad* wrote of two *sofrim* (scribes), one of whom was an expert calligrapher for *Sefer Torah* letters, but not as proficient at writing small letters in *tefillin*. The other *sofer* was not quite as good in the letters of his *Sifrei Torah*, but his skill was clearly superior in the writing of *tefillin*.

Our reaction might be: So what? *Rav Yosef Chaim* wrote: The specialized talent demonstrates that in one *sofer* the *neshamah*-aspect of his soul is primary, while in the other *sofer* the *nefesh*-aspect dominates; and, based on that diagnosis, each one should concentrate on certain *mitzvos* to develop his particular kind of soul. We may not know what all that means, but we see from it that no talent should be off-handedly disregarded as meaningless or trivial.

Even if it is not a talent, and has nothing to do with *mitzvos*, but is merely a hobby or an interest — if the child enjoys swimming, photography, hockey or birdwatching — is it all just a foolish waste of time? Sometimes time spent on unproductive activities may indeed be wasted, but the interest behind the activity should not be discounted as entirely foolish. The Gemara tells of a man who used to say: "If I could, I would build a palace near the sea." This man loved the sea, and spoke of it constantly. I would say, OK, everyone is entitled to his own *mishega'as*. But the Gemara says they checked and determined that this man was descended from *Shevet Zevulun,* from the tribe whose special blessing — whose service of Hashem — was intimately tied to the sea. This does not mean that every childish desire must be catered to. But every desire does reveal *something* about the child, and the wise parent is always on the lookout to discover more about this precious *neshamah* which has been given us to raise.

There is so much more to learn, such as the importance of *lo lishmah*, the fine art of correctly bribing children to train them to do what's right; or to learn how each child reacts differently to the prison that we adults call school, *cheder*, or *yeshivah ketanah*. The original Torah system ordained that children be taught programmed instruction at their own levels by their parents. Primary school was a reluctant concession made by our Sages, a compromise that affects a child in many ways, ways which need to be explored.

Consider the question of guidance in career planning: Would a *navi* tell *every* young man to enter a *kollel*? If so, then for how long? And when *Chovos HaLevavos* says that each person has a natural bent towards a certain occupation, how much freedom should children have to choose on their own and how do we distinguish between desire and whim?

Even if you never become an outstanding *navi*, and even if you never learn to read your child like a book, it is at least a beginning to be aware of all these ideas; to know that your child truly is a special soul, a unique combination of spiritual talent and blessing which never before existed and will never be again.

The *Alter of Slabodka* said that human beings cannot live without a certain amount of *kavod*, respect. I think he meant a certain amount of *self*-respect. We can help our children develop a healthy self-image, not by telling them they are better then others, but by helping them learn that he or she is precious and no one else can serve Hashem quite the way he or she can.

Our father Yaakov gave a special blessing to only two of his grandchildren, Ephraim and Menashe. Rav Yaakov Kamenetzky *z.l.* explained that they needed the blessing because they were born in Egypt, a foreign culture which might pull them away from Torah. What was the blessing? *The people of Israel will bless their children to become like you* (Genesis 48:20). Oddly, the blessing says nothing at all specific about Ephraim and Menashe!

Perhaps it means: Ephraim and Menashe, you do not have to copy Pharaoh or the Egyptians. You do not need to become like them or anyone else. Instead, develop the greatness that is in yourselves, and then others will strive to imitate *you*. Develop your special qualities, whatever they may be, and you will then become a source of blessing for everyone around you.

In all the work we put in, in all the good we attempt, we do not always see success and it can be discouraging. We should know that nothing good ever gets lost. King Eglon of Moav gave a little honor to the Torah, which at the time seemed to have no lasting effect. But our Sages say that it created a chain reaction, producing a convert named Ruth, then King David and many more links, ultimately leading to *Mashiach*. Surely, at least that much reward is waiting for every sincere Torah parent, that much and more.

Our father Avraham achieved such greatness in his life, including the honor of Hashem saying, *I love him* (Genesis 18:19). Why? Hashem did not give as His reason Avraham's *frumkeit*, and not even his *mesiras nefesh*. The love was because: *For he will command his children and his house after him, to keep the way of Hashem* (ibid.).

When we too make whatever little effort we can, we also become worthy of that love and that assistance from Heaven.

And as we work, we can also relax a bit inside, knowing that Avraham Avinu is up there being a *meilitz yosher,* putting in a good word for us, for those who can say: *"Zayde,* we have not forgotten, and we'll do our best not to let you down."

The Importance of Being Old

There are a number of commandments in the Torah relating to behavior regarding honor and reverence, e.g. the *mitzvos* of *yirah* (fear or reverence) to Hashem, to the *Beis HaMikdash* and to parents; and *mitzvos* to honor parents, Torah sages, *Kohanim* and the elderly. Most of these commandments are understandable enough, and virtually no one will argue against the principle of honoring Hashem, holy places, parents and *talmidei chachamim*.

However, the obligation to honor the elderly requires some analysis. Modern society admonishes, "Respect your elders," but how much respect is really given to them? Did you ever hear a commercial advertisement, "Drink Pepsi, for those who think old?" White hair-coloring is not a best-seller, and we don't compliment a friend's clothing by calling it "old-fashioned." So even if we do honor older people, society certainly does not give honor to Old Age.

Theoretically, we should ask ourselves: Why honor the elderly? If you were born in 1920, should you be respected more than someone born in 1950? Why should someone receive honors for a mere timing of birth?

This same question is even more perplexing in regard to the *mitzvah* to honor a *Kohen*. If one of your dinner guests happens to be a *Kohen*, you have a *mitzvah* to serve him the best portion. He may be a most ordinary fellow, but because he's descended from Aaron he receives the extra chicken-bone. Why should that be?

About 1900 years ago, the Gemara tells us, the Roman governor of *Eretz Yisrael*, Tyranus Rufus, asked the following question of Rabbi Akiva: "If *HaKadosh Baruch Hu* loves the poor, why doesn't *He* feed them?" Even if we will agree that once we are stuck with the needy it is a kindness to aid them, why did the Creator not create everyone to be self-sufficient, that others should not require our kindness in the first place? Rabbi Akiva replied: "In order to save us from the judgment of *Gehinnom*." The *mitzvah* of *tzedakah* is not primarily for the poor. It is for us, the donors, to afford us the opportunity to perform those *mitzvos* we need to qualify for entrance into the World to Come.

This statement is a key to unlock many doors. We tend to reason that since needy people exist, the Torah commands us to aid them; but Hashem could have arranged His universe in a way that there would be no needy people at all. We think that since human beings have parents, and parents are helpful things to have, the Torah tells us to honor them; but humans could have been created in a way that they would be born without the necessity for nurturing parents, as fish eggs or amoebae are created.

The *aleph beis* of *Yiddishkeit* is that the purpose of life is spiritual growth. We become elevated by giving *tzedakah*; therefore, Hashem created poor people to help us attain that elevation (why the poor people were chosen for this particular role is a question for another time). Honoring parents adds a dimension to our souls; therefore, *Rav Yerucham Levovitz* explained, we were given parents to give us that special spiritual dimension.

The general rule seems to be: In any *mitzvah* which requires us to give something to another person, the ultimate purpose of the *mitzvah* is not to benefit the other person, but to benefit ourselves.

It is a *mitzvah* to show respect to sages of the Torah. But perhaps a particular sage achieved greatness because he was blessed with a high I.Q. and there are other Jews less gifted who equally devote themselves to Torah. In the reward of the World to Come, isn't one tantamount to the other?

Probably, but even so, in the world we live in, our *mitzvah* is to honor the outstanding sage; not necessarily because he deserves it (although he usually does), but because *we* need it, we need to show this honor for our own benefit. *Rabbeinu Yonah* wrote that honoring the Torah sage is a way of demonstrating that Torah learning is important, a symbolic proclamation that the word of Hashem is indeed precious to us, and a goal to which we all aspire.

In *shul*, acting with decorum does not make the *Aron Kodesh* feel more worthy. My show of reverence (even if it's only a show) is for me; to help me learn to feel the sanctity and to learn to appreciate how special sanctity is. Even most of the prophets could not just sit down and tune in to the spirit of prophecy at will. They needed the appropriate atmosphere: tranquility, music and detachment from the mundane.

Rambam writes that the nearest thing to prophecy today is the elevation of true prayer. But successful *tefillah*, like prophecy, also needs atmosphere: tranquility, introspection, refraining from petty conversation and the awe of knowing that we stand in a holy place, *mikdash m'at,* the *Beis HaMikdash* in microcosm. Entering the *beis hak'nesses* without reverence is what enables us to mesh with the *kedushas beis hak'nesses,* and to carry away some of that *kedushah* with us when we depart.

This same concept helps us understand the *mitzvah* of honoring even the most mediocre *Kohen.* It has been said that the reason Hashem has not yet sent *Mashiach* is that He's waiting for us to request his arrival, to show that we really want him to come. So let's ask ourselves: What have we done, lately, to demonstrate that we are anxiously awaiting *Mashiach?*

There is something, at least one thing we do. Monday, Thursday and twice on Shabbos we read the Torah in *shul.* And the first person called for an *aliyah* is always a *Kohen.* Four times a week we publicly remind ourselves: Here is a man whose ancestors served in the *Beis HaMikdash.* Here is a man who will himself serve in the *Mikdash* when *Mashiach* comes, so let's honor him! Nineteen centuries since we last saw that *Mikdash*, we still honor its laid-off employees; that is how vital it is to us, how much we are still waiting to get it back. Nineteen centuries, and still showing loyalty, is a glory; not for the *Kohen,* but for us.

We honor the *shul,* and we come to feel the sanctity of the *shul.* We honor a *Kohen,* and we impress on ourselves the centrality of the *Beis HaMikdash.* We honor parents and we now comprehend; we thereby impress the importance of gratitude on ourselves, the need to feel indebted to those who gave us life and care. But why honor the elderly? If they are not relatives and their sole achievement is to have survived a long time, why should they be especially deserving of respect?

By now we know, at least in general, what the answer must be. This *mitzvah* of *kavod* is not necessary because old people need it, but because the young ones do. Since it is a *mitzvah,* it must be that every older person contains some lesson, some secret for us to learn. The elderly must symbolize something,

The Importance of Being Old □ 43

just as the *Kohen* symbolizes the *Mikdash* and the sage the Torah; and our *mitzvah* is to honor the elderly in order that we ourselves will learn to appreciate that symbol.

What is the symbol? What vital Torah message do older people carry around with them and convey to us?

It is possible to say that age represents wisdom, the knowledge of mature experience. *Pirkei Avos* says that forty is the age of understanding, and the ability to offer advice comes at fifty. However, the Gemara also tells us that wisdom is granted only to those who pursue it. "Those who do not seek Torah wisdom suffer mental atrophy and become progressively more foolish with age." Clearly, age in itself is by no means a yardstick for knowledge or perspicacity. But if not wisdom, what greatness does old age possess?

The answer (pointed out by *Rav Avigdor Miller, shlita*) is found in Gemara *Kiddushin*: "Rabbi Yochanan used to rise to honor even aged gentiles. He said: 'How many *harpatkai* (travails) have happened to them.'" Rashi explains the word *harpatkai*: "Many happenings and troubles, and they have seen many miracles and signs of Hashem's presence."

An elderly man, who has not studied Torah and is not even Jewish, has had many troubles, has seen many miracles. If he has seen miracles, he has seen signs, demonstrations of the presence of Hashem, that is what *Rashi* says.

Of the twenty-four Books of *Tanach*, the written Torah, there is one volume every *shul*-going Jew becomes acquainted with, one *sefer* he cannot avoid: *Tehillim*, the Book of Psalms. On Shabbos in *shul* we say over twenty chapters, and *shuls* that recite *Borchi Nafshi* say an additional sixteen. Whether or not we study them, *Tehillim* end up becoming an integral part of Jewish consciousness.

What is the central theme of *Tehillim*? It is on almost every page: *Give thanks to Hashem for He is good, for His kindness is eternal; He is King; Give to Hashem honor and might.* There are hundreds of variations on the theme that Hashem is truly in charge and He is truly good. Over a lifetime, a *shul*-going Jew reads close to half a million chapters of *Tehillim*. Those are enough pages to make a pile of *Tehillim* books, ninety feet high.

Those half-million chapters are necessary. We need all the decades it takes to say them, because it takes a long time before the lessons finally begin to sink in. It requires a lifetime to fully perceive that the Creator is *here*, and indeed, He *is* in charge, and truly, everything He does is always for the best.

That recognition, however, does not grow from the *siddur* alone. We must also get it from living. It takes years of observing the Divine Providence in our own lives, years of taking note of all the kindnesses. Most assuredly there will be years of asking questions, and raising discomforting contradictions. Then there must come still more years, to answer the questions, to resolve the contradictions and perhaps to realize that they did not exist in the first place.

As *Tehillim* says (14:15), *The righteous still blossom in old age . . . To relate that Hashem is righteous and there is no crookedness in Him* (*Psalms* 92:15). It is the elderly who come to true, heartfelt understanding that Hashem is always in the right, that it is He Who supports us, and all He does is for the best — those are lessons which take a long time to learn. In old age, those who have suffered the vicissitudes of life are the ones, who are equipped to shout: *For His kindness is eternal.*

As *Rabbi Yochanan* put it: How many *harpatkai* have passed over the old! And as *Rashi* explained: So many troubles and miracles for every person; and signs of Divine Presence in their lives. Only the elderly see them, because they have lived long, and have traveled the length of life's river; and it is they who understand that, in the end, the river leads down to the sea.

About thirty years ago, my wife's *zayde*, Mr. Levy z.l., attended the wedding of a grandchild where he met the Lakewood Rosh Yeshivah. Old Mr. Levy told him: "I learned long ago that *HaKadosh Baruch Hu* knows His business better than I do. But I am now learning that He also knows *my* business better than I do."

When I married ten years later, Mr. Levy was no longer living, but the Lakewood Rosh Yeshivah repeated it to me. *Im yirtzeh Hashem,* after 120 years when I finally get to meet Mr. Levy, I will want to stand up to honor him; because he taught me a lesson that can be taught only by one who has been through the mill, seeing the difficulties, and also the miracles, into a ripe old age.

Not every elderly person sees the miracles, they do not all recognize the Hand of Hashem. The old gentiles mentioned in the Gemara were no different from gentiles today, but Rabbi Yochanan stood up for them anyway. Even if they do not appreciate Divine Providence, even if they never understood that the Creator supported them, Rabbi Yochanan still wanted to honor them; not for their sake, but for his own.

Just as we honor the *Kohen* and the synagogue, to teach ourselves reverence for the *Beis HaMikdash* and *beis hak'nesses,* so too we honor the elderly, those who have experienced the full range of Hashem's relationship, in order to impress ourselves with the importance of what that relationship is, and the importance of us experiencing it too.

Every older person is someone who has had the chance to know the Master of the Universe, someone who was shown the miracles. Did they use their opportunity? That's irrelevant. What is important is that *we* use the opportunity, to honor the person who has lived with Divine Providence so long, in order to awaken ourselves to the idea of seeing Divine Providence in our own lives. If in honoring them we remind ourselves of the importance of observing Hashem's plan, to acknowledge that everything is from Heaven and it's all to the good, then we have given meaning to old age, to theirs and to ours.

Eighty years ago in China, when meeting someone for the first time, etiquette demanded that your opening question was: "And what is your glorious age?" If he replied, "Twenty-five," you had to respond sympathetically and say, "Well, someday you will be older." If he was over thirty, one responded with a gesture of respect. If forty, that was indeed enviable. And if he was past fifty! After fifty years he was considered so venerable that he was permitted to grow a beard, as a sign of authority.

That's the spirit! (Of course, Jewish men are entitled to grow beards even before they're fifty.) We need to develop this same reverence, this respect for each additional year of living with Hashem's kindness, another decade of observing the Divine pattern. It is the elderly themselves who should lead the way. The term "senior citizen" is a patronizing euphemism. An old man is a *zaken* and an old woman a *zekeinah*, "an old one," and they should be proud of it; because only they can have the complete perspective on this world, a perspective all of us should hope to share.

A side benefit of being over seventy is that you can make all kinds of statements (outrageous and otherwise) to people and get away with it. Even if you don't live in an Orthodox neighborhood, walk into a Jewish-owned store and tell the salesman: "Isn't it a beautiful day G-d gave us?" When he nods his head, say: "Let's go together to *shul* this Friday night, to give thanks for the beautiful days." Try it! You'll discover a new hobby.

But even those of us who are not yet seventy can still begin; by counting our blessings, by noticing what Hashem does for us and by getting used to the idea that Hashem truly does know our business better than we do; and old age, with training, instead of a period of decline, can be an era of spiritual greatness for us and everyone we meet.

In Search of Our Teacher Moshe

It has been said that only we Jews could re-tell an epic adventure story, year after year, without ever making mention of the main character. The story, our Exodus from Egypt, is faithfully retold from the *Haggadah* every Pesach at the *Seder*, a *Seder* at which the name of the main character — Moshe Rabbeinu, our teacher Moshe — is noticeably absent.

Commentators explain that Moshe's name is omitted in order to remind us that the true Hero of the Exodus was

Hashem, and our greatest thanks must be reserved for the One Who set us free with His Mighty Hand and Outstretched Arm. Even so, especially at Pesach time or when reading the *sidros* (weekly portions of the Torah) dealing with Egypt, it is proper to take time to consider the life story of our great teacher; not only because gratitude is due him, but because Moshe's life is intended to provide a spiritual yardstick for all of us. "Every person is fit to become a *tzaddik* like Moshe Rabbeinu" (*Rambam*), which means that every person has an obligation to make the attempt.

Stories are recorded in the Torah not merely to teach ancient history, but to teach us necessary lessons about ourselves. They are meant to give direction and help in overcoming life's obstacles, and guidance in the search for meaning and personal Torah growth every day. But therein lies a problem.

Moshe Rabbeinu is to be our role-model. But *no prophet arose like him* (*Deuteronomy* 34:10). He was *the humblest of all men* (*Numbers* 12:3). Midrashim tell us that he looked like an angel of God, and he was utterly without fear (*Midrash HaGadol*). The *Zohar* compares Moshe and Mount Sinai to iron and a magnet. Awesome, yes, and inspiring; but what does that have to do with people like us? What is the sense of trying to follow in the footsteps of an angel? Our teacher Moshe is the central human figure in *Chumash*; but as a human being, "this *man* Moshe" is totally beyond our ken, beyond any possibility of relating to him or emulating him.

However, since Moshe's life is recorded for us to follow, there must be some way we can connect our lives to his, to become students of our great teacher. The Torah provides a clue. In the stories of the Patriarchs, and almost all the saintly personalities in *Chumash*, these men and women are presented to us as "finished products," without any explanation of how they became saintly in the first place. The Midrash tells of our father Avraham's childhood, but *Chumash* itself does not take real notice until Avraham becomes a prophet, worthy to hear the voice of Hashem. How Avraham achieved this, the struggles and the setbacks, go unmentioned.

The story of Moshe Rabbeinu, the eternal role-model, is more complete. We all know how Moshe was placed in a basket on the river, adopted by Pharaoh's daughter and nursed by his own mother. The first detail the Torah mentions about him after his infancy, the source of all that came afterwards, was: *Moshe grew up and went out to his brothers, and looked upon their burdens* (*Exodus* 2:11). Moshe appears to have been a compassionate soul from the very beginning, a loyal son of his people, as if he had been born with a nobility of spirit far beyond anything we might hope to attain.

However, the usual translation "he looked upon their burdens" is not quite correct. The Torah says: *He looked* into *their burdens*. What does it mean to look into a burden? *Rashi* explains, quoting *Midrash Rabbah*: "He placed his eyes and his heart to feel pain for them." Moshe spent time observing his brothers, seeing their suffering, and he placed his heart, he concentrated his thoughts, on *trying* to feel their pain.

The Torah is teaching us something revolutionary. Moshe Rabbeinu was not born an angel, he was not created with a natural river of flowing compassion. Instead, we are told the secret of his spiritual success, the beginning from which all else followed: He took time *to learn to feel* the other person's pain. It was not natural empathy, for Moshe had been raised in a palace; but he worked at it, straining to understand what his brothers felt, trying to see *into* their burden. The Midrash says he literally put himself in their place, making bricks together with them to experience what it meant to be enslaved, what it meant to be a child of Israel in the land of Egypt.

To work on empathy, to make a serious effort to develop an appreciation for what the other fellow is going through, that was Moshe's first step; and it is a step all of us can try to take.

Besides being his first-mentioned quality, is there any evidence that this empathy was Moshe's most *outstanding* quality? There is. The Midrash says that Hashem chose Moshe after observing how he took care of his father-in-law's sheep. A young lamb ran away from the flock, and Moshe exhausted himself in a long pursuit, until he finally caught up with the animal when it stopped to drink some water. He said: "So that's what you wanted! I didn't know you were thirsty. You must be tired from all the running. Let me give you a ride home on my shoulder." And he carried the lamb back to its flock.

Hashem said: "Moshe, you know how to care for the lambs, you are the one to care for My people." This does not mean that to be a Jewish leader you must go to veterinarian school. It means that after the long chase, Moshe said to the lamb: "You must be tired." The lamb is tired? What about Moshe? Another shepherd might have vented his exhaustion on the animal. But Moshe had trained himself to put himself in the other's place. Even if it is only a sheep, how does the sheep feel? Surely it's tired, and Moshe's mind was not focused on his own tiredness, there were more important things to think about — *that* is how one is chosen as a shepherd, to lead the people of *HaKadosh Baruch Hu.*

This same greatness of intellectual and emotional identification with others which we find at the onset of Moshe's career, we also encounter at its ending. When his time came to die, Moshe requested of Hashem to appoint as his successor a man of *ruach*, of spirit. *Rashi* explains that it means: a man who understands that each person's individual spirit is different, and a man who can cope with each individual according to his particular needs. Those were the qualities possessed by Moshe's successor Yehoshua, because they were the outstanding qualities of Moshe himself.

The more we learn about our teacher, the more we find this same theme running through the story of his life, again and again: making the effort to put himself in the other person's sandals, which enabled him to communicate with the other person, and to grow ever greater himself.

A simple example, one from which we ourselves can learn: The Midrash says that Moshe wanted to persuade Pharaoh to give his Israelite slaves a day of rest. Did he appeal to Pharaoh on humanitarian grounds? Of course not. Instead, he told him: Our present system is not cost effective; we are over-straining the work force. Overall productivity would increase if the slaves were given one day a week to recuperate. Moshe Rabbeinu stooped to put himself in Pharaoh's place, and with Pharaonic thinking he persuaded him to let the children of Israel off for Shabbos.

True empathy, which can make both a compassionate *tzaddik* and a successful salesman, can also make someone an expert in getting along with relatives. Putting ourselves in another's place to perceive his or her viewpoint will show us what needs to be said to communicate most effectively. When Hashem told Moshe to leave his father-in-law Yisro and return to Egypt, Moshe did not tell Yisro, "The Lord appeared to me." Instead, he said that he wanted to visit his brothers, to see them once again. *Midrash HaGadol* explains that Moshe was not lying, but he chose the reason Yisro would most easily believe and appreciate. One must communicate a message in a manner the listener is able to digest.

When Moshe delivered Divine warnings in Pharaoh's palace, the Torah says *he turned and he walked out* (*Exodus* 10:6). Why does it mention that he turned? *Midrash Rabbah* explains: Moshe turned to look at the Egyptians, and saw that his message was getting through; so he left immediately to allow them to seize the moment to discuss it among themselves and perhaps they would repent. Most people who begin to speak are difficult to turn off, but Moshe was thinking only of the benefit to his listeners; he was attuned to picking up cues, from facial expressions and body language, and he knew when to stop speaking and leave.

Moshe foretold the tenth plague, warning Egypt that Hashem would strike its first-born *at about midnight.* The Gemara asks why he said, "*about* midnight"; was he unsure of Hashem's arrival time, that He might be late? The Gemara answers that Hashem would surely come at the stroke of midnight, but Moshe's concern was: If the Egyptian timepieces were running a little fast, they might think that midnight had already arrived and yet there was no plague! Even if the plague hit five minutes later, it would lose some of its psychological impact; so Moshe said, "*about* midnight," give or take a few minutes.

Moshe is telling them Divine Truth; must he make allowances for their petty miscalculations? We see here that indeed he must. Even in teaching Torah we must take into account the frailty of the individual listener, to say what he will be able to hear, that teaching should not be counter-productive. To do this you must be able to figure out how the other person thinks, even if the other person is an Egyptian pharaoh.

After the construction of the *Mishkan*, or Tabernacle in the wilderness, Moshe gave the people of Israel a detailed accounting of how every penny that had been donated was allocated. Would anyone have the *chutzpah* to accuse Moshe Rabbeinu of embezzling funds? But Moshe understood people's minds, and he wished to remove any remote possibility of suspicion. He also adopted a policy of never accepting any gift or personal favor from anyone; because he knew that when the chips were down, as at Korach's rebellion, no matter how sincere he was, if personal gain was involved, he could not expect others to trust quite so readily.

Moshe was the humblest man on earth, but he did not make the mistake of expecting others to be humble too. He put himself in their place, and was able to feel their special sensitivities. When it came time to select the seventy judges of the first Sanhedrin, he had each tribe send six representatives, and the seventy-two delegates drew lots to determine which two would be excluded from the final seventy. Moshe could have chosen the seventy himself, but he did not, because he said: If I chose six judges from ten tribes and only five judges from the other two tribes, their feelings will be hurt.

Hurt feelings? This is a fulfillment of the command of Hashem; how petty can one be!? But Moshe understood: As noble as humility is, and however humble you are, if you assume that the other fellow is supersensitive, you won't go wrong. Moshe also planned the *Mishkan's* inauguration to take twelve days, so that each tribe would have a day in the limelight. In dealing with the *nesiim*, the princes of each tribe,

Targum Yonasan says that Moshe would sometimes pretend not to know the answer to a question, that they might learn not to be ashamed to admit when they themselves did not know.

Moshe Rabbeinu took care not to cause even Yehoshua, his disciple and personal servant, to feel inferior. In telling Yehoshua to select soldiers to war against Amalek, Moshe said, *Choose men for us* (*Exodus* 17:9), for both of us, as if they were equals. Yehoshua was both student and servant, but you don't have to unnecessarily remind your employee that he takes orders from you.

He empathized, even with his enemies. To effectively handle a complaint of a personal attack we must ask ourselves, what does this person really want? What makes him tick? When Korach and company came with all sorts of wild accusations, Moshe replied "We will see in the *morning*," tomorrow. The Midrash says that Moshe was thinking, "Perhaps they became excited after too much eating and drinking, and may reconsider, overnight." Because of this delay one of the ringleaders, Ohn ben Peles, did reconsider, and his life was saved. Through it all, Moshe did not lose himself; he knew how to tune in to the other fellow's wavelength and to relate to him.

This sublime quality came to the fore in one of the most heroic acts in all history: Moshe's prayer for the Children of Israel after the sin of the Golden Calf. The nation had sinned, and Hashem said: Moshe, let Me wipe them out, and I shall make of you and your children a new nation.

Can we imagine the temptation involved in this offer? The people had given Moshe trouble all along, and they did not even show him the courtesy to await his return from Sinai one extra day before making the Golden Calf. Here was an opportunity to create a new holy people, from his own family! Even more tempting, Moshe's own children were not worthy enough to succeed him as leaders (*Avos d'R' Nosson* 17:3). Accepting Hashem's offer would virtually guarantee Divine assistance to assure that Moshe's sons would be great *tzaddikim*. How could any parent respond except to say, Your Will be done, and let the sinners perish?

But Moshe had trained himself to think of the "other," and at this point he thought, What is in *Hashem's* Mind, right now? If He wishes to destroy Israel, let Him do so; why must He tell me about it? (*Midrash Rabbah* 42:9). And Moshe realized that Hashem's desire was for him to reject the offer, and instead pray for forgiveness, which he did; so much so that he said, *If You destroy them, wipe me out along with them* (*Exodus* 32:32).

Wonder of wonders, the Midrash says that Moshe Rabbeinu, with all his sanctity, was yet able to place himself into the shoes of the sinner, to give Hashem every conceivable excuse to forgive. "Hashem, You took us out of Egypt, where idols were worshiped by everybody. You gave us lots of gold, which is always a source of trouble, and You phrased the Ten Commandments in the singular, as if You were speaking only to me and not them. Also, at Sinai they were frightened and stood far off, and cannot be blamed if the message did not sink in."

These were all sinners' rationalizations, which Moshe, more than anyone, knew were far from adequate; still, he put himself in the sinners' place to such a degree that the Midrash says, "Hashem did not know what to answer!" Surely the Almighty could have given an answer. But it means that since Moshe in all his holiness could yet feel so much for the sinners, so completely was he able to identify with their weakness, that in the end *HaKadosh Baruch Hu* had no choice but to do likewise and forgive them.

We have seen how Moshe Rabbeinu's empathy led him to understand other people, and to be able to deal with them and lead them, and even to defend them before the Divine Judge. But Moshe was much more than just a kind, loving human being. He was also the greatest of the prophets, and Rambam writes that attaining prophecy requires the greatest amount of wisdom. What was the source of Moshe's wisdom, that it surpassed all others?

Midrash Shochar Tov answers: Moshe was the greatest of the prophets because he begged mercy from Hashem for the sake of Israel. What connection is there between prayer for a fellow Jew and the gift of prophecy?

The Gemara says that the difference between Moshe and the other prophets was that the others saw a vision of Hashem through a clouded window, while Moshe saw his vision through a clear, shining lens [אספקלריא המאירה]. *Sefarim* explain that we do not see visions of Hashem, not because He is hiding, but because our thoughts are so focused on something else that there is no place for Hashem's presence to truly enter. What is this something else that occupies our thoughts twenty-four hours a day?

It is: Ourselves. I, me and mine are the most fascinating words in everyone's vocabulary. When I meet another person, I am less interested in them than I am in the impression *I* am making on them: How do I look? Are they listening to me? How should I respond to what they say? In the same way, each of us has a window facing Hashem, but we have painted over our windows to transform them into mirrors, so that we see nothing but ourselves.

The *navi* (prophet) is the man or woman who has managed to rise above this limitation, to make contact with the Divine. However, even a *navi* has some ego, some small speck of self-interest and self-absorption to smudge the glass and cloud the window. But Moshe Rabbeinu, who trained himself from earliest years to take his mind off himself to think about others, was the one who could see others clearly and truly care for them; and therefore he was also the one who could look at Hashem without subjective static, without ego, and through his clear window became the greatest prophet of them all.

Moshe was also greatest in knowledge of Torah. Here too, we find a direct link between Torah wisdom and empathy, that learning to think about others makes one a better student. *Mishnah Avos* tells us that one of the forty-eight prerequisites for Torah wisdom is bearing the yoke with a friend, which means to learn to feel a friend's pain, and also his joy. Rav Avraham Grodzensky of Slabodka was once seen to be in an unusually joyous mood and, when asked why, explained that a friend was getting married in another city. Though he was unable to attend in person, he could at least share the *simchah*, to literally feel the happiness his friend was experiencing at the same time, albeit in a different place.

How are we to understand this, that sharing another's joy and sorrow is a factor in attaining excellence in Torah learning? Rav Simcha Zissel Ziv explained: Torah development means learning to comprehend that which we do not yet comprehend; and true learning, not only the accumulation of additional facts but new perspectives, requires us to step *outside* ourselves, to look at the subject from a new point of view.

It takes great effort to even *hear* an explanation that differs with one's preconceived notions, and even greater effort to focus in depth on both sides of a *machlokes* (dispute). "Why did Tosafos interpret the Gemara in a different manner than I did? How would Rashi reply to Tosafos' argument? Why would Tosafos not be satisfied with such a reply?" We must rise above our limitations, to try to climb the shoulders of giants to dimly perceive what they so clearly saw.

Ultimately, all Torah learning is an attempt to tune into the thoughts of the Divine, a knowledge which is superhuman. As Rav Boruch Ber Leibowitz said, The Torah of Hashem cannot be approached with mere human logic; the approach itself must be with Torah ways of reasoning, to enter a higher plane of mind. Basic training for this mental elevation, *Avos* tells us, is to learn to move beyond ourselves by learning to bear the yoke of a friend.

If someone does attain this sublime level, he or she will discover that it is not a denial of self, not a loss of one's individual mind. To the contrary, their ability to make a crucial decision on their own expands. Our Sages tell us that when Moshe Rabbeinu saw the Golden Calf, he smashed the tablets of the Ten Commandments *on his own initiative.* How could any flesh-and-blood take it upon himself to destroy the Tablets given by the Creator, without first asking?

Moshe Rabbeinu's mind was so attuned to Divine thinking that he no longer needed to ask; he already knew. Hashem told him afterwards: More power to you for smashing them, it was the correct decision. Only someone whose mind is totally focused on truth could make such a choice; but Moshe possessed that objectivity and wisdom, because he had learned to move outside himself from the start, when he trained his thoughts to look into others' burdens and to feel them.

We have learned that Moshe Rabbeinu's empathy is the key to understanding his greatness as a *tzaddik*, a leader, a prophet, and a teacher of Torah. Emulating him as best we can by making an effort to feel for others and put ourselves in their places will certainly help us also to become more righteous, more learned, and more proficient in getting along with everyone we meet. But there remains one question which needs to be answered, a question most of us have never heard asked: Was Moshe Rabbeinu *happy*? Being a perfect *tzaddik* and a paragon of self-sacrifice, did he enjoy his life?

Such questions, posed sincerely, are not at all disrespectful, and they are important to ask; because, inspiring as the life of an idealist may be, we will never seek to emulate him if we think it means giving up everything we hold dear. We may revere the suffering saint, we may honor the *tzaddik* who gives his all for the Jewish people, but we don't generally want him to rub off on us. So: Did Moshe have an enjoyable life? Was he a happy man?

The answer is, clearly, that he was.

Rav Yosef Yoizel Horvitz of Novardok was walking with one of his disciples when they passed two teenagers, a non-Jewish girl and boy, who were embracing and laughing together. Rav Horvitz turned to his student and said: "Do you think those two have found happiness? I assure you, their laughter is only to mask their inner sorrow." Rav Horvitz did not explain his words at the time, but as he continued to walk he added in a whisper, as if speaking to himself, "I have known in my life but one truly happy man, and that was Rav Yisrael Salanter."

Anyone who has heard of Rav Yisrael Salanter knows he was outstanding in piety, in learning, in nobility of character and in self-sacrifice. All his years were spent in poverty, he enjoyed none of the material pleasures, and he had no private life, giving up everything to work for the Jewish people. A holy *tzaddik*, certainly; but how could Rav Horvitz say that Rav Yisrael was the *happiest* of men in his own lifetime?

To return to Moshe Rabbeinu for a parallel: He was the most saintly of all men, and the most self-sacrificing, and we find in the Torah that he had a most difficult life. After Pharaoh tried to kill him, he wandered as a fugitive for many years. Even after he found safety in Midian, what was it like for one who had grown up a prince to now be a shepherd? After Hashem appeared to him, the situation did not improve. In their first conversation Moshe said something he shouldn't have, and as a result forever lost the chance to become a *Kohen*. On the road to Egypt he made another mistake, and an angel almost killed him.

He came to Pharaoh, and Pharaoh threw him out. For six months (the *Ramban* explains) nothing happened except that Jewish suffering increased, Moshe was blamed for it and his people cursed him. All this time in Egypt, he was separated from his wife and children.

After the Exodus, Moshe endured forty years of complaints concerning food and drink, the Golden Calf and the spies in Korach's rebellion. Sometimes, people even threw stones at him, and the Midrash says that they often spoke ill of him. If Moshe left home early in the morning, tongues wagged that he must be fighting with his wife. When his sister took sick his prayers had to be brief, for otherwise people would accuse him of caring for his sister and not for others. They accused him of nepotism, they accused him of causing the deaths of innocent people, and they even accused him of insanity.

It was not easy creating the nation of Hashem from scratch. At the end of it all, his personal desire, that his son might succeed him, did not materialize, and his children did not develop as he had hoped. But after all this, we proclaim in the *davening*, every Shabbos: "Moshe *rejoiced*."

Perhaps he rejoices only now, from his place in Heaven, but not back then while he lived? Consider the evidence: After forty years of hard labor, when Moshe handed the reins of leadership over to Yehoshua, *Midrash Rabbah* says that he told him, "They are still a young people, do not become upset by what they do." If Moshe said it, it means that he felt it; there was no bitterness, and no burnout, even after forty years.

He had lost his chance to be a *Kohen*. But *Midrash Rabbah* says that when he saw Aaron anointed with the oil of consecration to become the *Kohen Gadol* (High Priest), Moshe was as happy as if he himself had been the anointed one.

Can you picture what it is like to live a life so free of envy that another person's success gives you as much joy as your own?

Hashem commanded Moshe to go to Pharaoh together with the Elders, but the Midrash says that when the time came, each of the Elders suddenly remembered that he had a previous appointment. They were understandably frightened, and Moshe went on to Pharaoh without them. He not only went, but *Midrash HaGadol* says he went "without fear."

Can you picture what it is like to live a life of doing the right thing and never feeling afraid?

The Torah says that when Aaron pointed out that Moshe had committed an error in *halachah*, Moshe admitted his mistake publicly. *Targum Yonasan* adds that he sent out a public message, "I was in error, and Aaron corrected me." That takes a great deal of courage; but for Moshe Rabbeinu it was somewhat easier to tell the truth, because *Toras Kohanim* says he admitted his mistake without embarrassment.

Can you imagine living a life so much at peace with yourself that you can publicly admit your mistakes without any embarrassment? The Torah tells us still more: "It was *good* in his eyes." Moshe was happy to be corrected, because that is how we learn.

So we see before us a man who gave his entire life without receiving even a thank-you, but who was free from all bitterness; a man who was free from envy, and enjoyed another person's success as if it was his own; a man who did what needs doing even when no one else would join in, and who faced mighty Pharaoh without fear; and a man who was able to admit his errors without embarrassment, publicly and cheerfully, "it was good in his eyes."

Literally, the Hebrew *Yismach Moshe* of the Sabbath should be translated in the future tense — Moshe *will* rejoice — indicating an ongoing, continual joy without end. That is why Rav Horvitz said that Rav Yisrael Salanter was a happy man. He was not of Moshe's caliber — no one is — but for a man of our generations, Rav Yisrael was free of envy, anger, pride, lust and fear; and he was happy, not because of things he possessed, but because of all the things he was.

How did Moshe achieve all this, where did the happiness come from? The answer is clear enough; it came from the same source of all his greatness — *vayar besivlosam* (*Exodus* 2:11) — the time spent training himself to feel for others and put himself in their place.

As a result of his training, he understood the underlying anxieties of people who complained and cursed, and he could deal with them without feeling frustrated or disgusted. Since he had learned to literally feel another's joy, he could take pleasure in Aaron's appointment without pangs of envy, even if the appointment was one he had desired for himself. On account of the fact that he had ceased to focus on himself, because his interest was in Hashem's will rather than self-interest, his mind had no room for fear or embarrassment; his thoughts were busy elsewhere, bound up in the greatness of the adventure in which he was continually engaged.

An American writer once noted that, to a true professional, work is very much like play; he is relaxed and in control, knowing his job and doing it without strain. Moshe Rabbeinu was a true professional, in the profession of living. That is why he could speak harshly to Pharaoh to admonish him, and at the same time (the Midrash points out) he would phrase his words in a respectful manner. His composure saved him from becoming flustered when Korach agitated; and instead of giving a direct answer, Moshe recognized the real trouble, and responded to the underlying emotion to try to diffuse the situation.

This same composure explains why, even after being informed of his own imminent death, Moshe was still able to think of the needs of others, to create cities of refuge for those guilty of manslaughter, and to ask Hashem to appoint a successor so that Israel would not be leaderless. Even Moshe's dying was the fulfillment of a Divine command — *Moshe the servant of Hashem died there . . . by the command of Hashem* (*Deuteronomy* 34:5) — because all his living was geared to the Divine command; and therefore the Gemara says that even his passing was in joy, with a Divine kiss.

We can never truly fathom Moshe's awesome greatness. But the goal of our Torah-study is not so much to understand Moshe as it is to understand ourselves, the Moshe Rabbeinu that *Rambam* tells us each of us could become. *Midrash Rabbah* adds that "there is no generation without a Moshe," and his life is eternally inscribed in the Torah to give us hope that we can emulate him; not just by feeling for others, but by working to *train* ourselves to feel the noble emotions we do not yet feel naturally, to leave the comfort of our private palaces, to put our minds to other's burdens, and also to their joys.

And also, perhaps, to take a moment to imagine what it is like to *have* an intense feeling for *mitzvos*, what it's like to be a *tzaddik* with an intense relationship with *HaKadosh Baruch Hu*. You can carry the burden, even with yourself, by mentally picturing the sublime self you *could* be, the self you were meant to be, and, with help from Hashem, the self you will someday indeed become.

Something for Satan

In considering all the various *middos* (character) problems in human relations, and *middos* problems in general, the older one becomes the more one realizes how truly difficult it is to effect any worthwhile personal change at all. *Rav Yisrael Salanter* said that it is easier to learn (or did he say it is easier to know?) all *Shas*, the entire Talmud, than to change one trait of character. So for most of us little people, what should we do? If you are someone in whom the *yetzer hara* (evil inclination) is clearly dominant over the *yetzer hatov* (good inclination), what practical approach is there to do something about it?

Permit me to share an insight with you based on *Divrei Yehoshua*, by Rav Yisrael Salanter's disciple, Rav Yehoshua Heller. The Torah commands us to love Hashem *with all your heart* (*Deuteronomy* 6:5), which the Gemara explains to mean, "with both your inclinations."

Some people assume this refers only to unique *tzaddikim*, such as our father Avraham — who our Sages tell us made peace with his *yetzer hara* — who use even negative emotions for holy purposes. But the commandment is addressed to all of us, which means that to some extent every person is capable of serving Hashem by using his or her individual *yetzer hara*. If you happen to be endowed with an active vigorous, world-class *yetzer hara*, then who knows? You might be just the person who can most benefit from using him.

For instance, *Mishlei* says that *Stolen water is sweet* (*Proverbs* 9:17), a classic example of the power of the *Satan* (another name for the *yetzer hara*). Something completely tasteless, like water, becomes attractive once it's forbidden. However, the Gemara says that this evil power was once used for good. There was a wicked man, a suspected adulterer, who nevertheless ran a risk in order to save the life of the husband of the woman he was involved with. The Gemara suggests the reason he saved the husband: If the husband died, then the affair would no longer be sinful. If it's no sin, then why carry on with it, since only *stolen* water is sweet? So in order to keep matters illicit, the *yetzer hara* pushed the sinner to save his rival's life. It was wickedness, but a wickedness which in its own perverse way led to some good.

Now, how can you and I use this power of the *yetzer*, every day? You probably know the story of the *tzaddik* who awoke early in the morning to go to the *Beis HaMidrash,* and along came that little voice we all know, which said: "It is so early! You need your sleep, stay in bed." The *tzaddik* replied: "*Satan*, you have convinced me. But instead of the *Beis HaMidrash,* what if I get up now to go to the theater, catch the early show, or maybe get in a little fishing?" The little voice chuckles, "Now you're talking!" And the *Satan* helped him out of bed, got him dressed in a hurry, pushed him out the door — but, since the fellow was a *tzaddik* after all, once he was out of the house, instead of going to the theater, he ran to the *Beis HaMidrash*.

Is negotiating with one's *yetzer hara* in this manner demeaning? Not so, because our Sages tell us that King David used to do it. This simple technique can help make life at least a little easier for all of us. If it's difficult to get up for a *mitzvah* in the morning, then imagine that you have something pleasurable to do which is not a *mitzvah*, not so spiritual, and you will find it easier to escape the pull of the mattress. Once you are up anyway, you may as well do whatever *mitzvah* activity you had originally planned. The rule is: We can seldom hope to vanquish the *yetzer hara*. Instead, we must try to trick him into helping us.

To make full use of one's *yetzer*, Rav Heller writes that one of the most effective tools is to use *ga'avah*, foolish, egotistical pride. Pride is childish, and we succumb to its temptations only because of the *Satan*. But if you've got it, why not use it, for good? For example, if you wish to begin a new *mitzvah* project, e.g. smiling at your in-laws or not speaking *lashon hara* till after 10 a.m., but you have no will power, how can the *yetzer hara* be of help?

In London, England, there stood an imposing old structure called the Admiralty Building, headquarters of the British Navy. The structure was not originally intended for the Navy or for any branch of government. How did this come about? The architect in charge of designing naval headquarters mixed up his blueprints. When the day came for him to show the proposed design to Queen Victoria, he inadvertently showed her a blueprint for a new asylum for the insane.

The queen, not knowing the difference, gave royal approval, and then what was the poor architect to do? Should he go back and tell her, "So sorry, your highness, but the plans I just showed your majesty are not for the Navy, they're for the hospital?" His pride was at stake, *ga'avah*; so he had no choice but to follow through, and the asylum blueprint was used to construct what became the British naval headquarters for many years to come.

The *Satan* is not confined to London; you can use the same technique wherever you are. You wish to abstain from *lashon hara* — let people know about it! Tell your friends, your rabbi, your mother-in-law, put an ad in the Jewish paper boasting of your new resolution. Then, next time you feel tempted to let something slip, the *yetzer hara* of pride will warn you: Others are watching you, you better keep to your resolution, or else you are in a heap of trouble.

Another useful form of pride is to delude yourself into believing that you have a reputation to live up to. Most people delude themselves anyway, all the time, so you may as well get some mileage out of it. My older brother came from out-of-town to visit, and he commented on how calm I was in dealing with my children. Should I have confessed the truth, that the kids had run me so ragged that I was too exhausted to yell? So I just smiled politely — but a moment later, when the baby overturned the sugar bowl, you should have seen how calm I was! I had to be, my fan club was watching.

So if you can think of yourself as dignified, and tranquil, and superior — all *ga'avah*, perhaps, conceited lies — the next time people start hollering at the committee meeting, you can tell yourself: I cannot lose my cool, my reputation is at stake. This is what we call petty pride — and it's useful.

If you prefer to major in egotism, the really heavy *shtusim* (foolishness), you can practice thinking like the fool depicted in *Mesillas Yesharim* who says: "I am so lofty, so distinguished, that I no longer need honors or recognition from the plebeians. It is certainly beneath my dignity to lose my temper. In fact, after possessing so many other outstanding qualities, I might as well also become famous for my humility, and I shall give *in* to the other fellow to show them all how saintly I truly am." Unfortunately, after a while this sort of attitude begins to let off an unpleasant stench, so ersatz humility is not a good long-term investment. But in the short run, if you do attend committee meetings or have argumentative relatives, it often pays to get the *yetzer* to help you, if he can.

So much for pride. What about *sinah*, true hatred, and *nekamah*, the desire for vengeance? Those are the *Satan's* heavy artillery; but if we are stuck with them, we may as well use them to help. I once knew an observant Jew who had an enemy, someone for whom he nursed an almost pathological hatred. He told me: "I hate that guy; but I won't speak badly of him. Because *Chovos HaLevavos* says, if you speak ill of someone, Hashem makes it up to the victim and he gets rewarded in the World to Come. So I'm not going to speak any *lashon hara* about him, because I want to make sure he burns in *Gehinnom* forever!"

It was a tragic case. But then again, if hatred keeps you from speaking *lashon hara*, it's something of a *nechamah*, a consolation. You do not have to work to develop a fiery hate, certainly nothing more than you already have. Even if you possess merely a little resentment, you can tell yourself: "Shall I speak about *him*, and show that he bothers me? Should I give him the satisfaction of giving me ulcers? Never!"

A woman who had been through a messy divorce asked a newspaper advice-columnist what to do when she meets her ex-husband's new wife at a social gathering. The reply was that she should be perfectly charming and friendly, in order to make the other woman feel guilty; and also to subtly convey sympathy that the second wife had gotten stuck with an old fool of a husband. Politeness to our enemies to hurt them is not a virtue, but it sure beats being *impolite* for the same purpose.

Even more powerful than hate is *nekamah*, the desire for revenge. As *Mesillas Yesharim* writes, for one who desires vengeance, nothing else will give peace. But even the desire for *nekamah* can be sublimated into a *mitzvah*. In the last generation there was a *tzaddik* who became famous for his *hachnasas orchim*, hospitality to guests. What was it that inspired him to excel in this particular *mitzvah* above all others?

According to his biographer (Ruchama Shain, in *All for the Boss*), when he was thirteen years old in turn-of-the-century Manhattan, his immigrant parents had to return to Eastern Europe without him. He had a menial job paying a dollar twenty-five a week, and his parents arranged for him to receive room and board with relatives in the city for a dollar a week. One Friday afternoon, shortly after his parents had left the country, the relatives told the boy that they had changed their minds; instead of a dollar every week, they were going to charge him a dollar twenty-five.

The thirteen-year-old boy rushed out to the street in tears, and spent that Shabbos alone in Central Park. It was a Shabbos of bitterness and misery — but the boy promised himself that when he grew up, when *he* had a home of his own, no one else was going to suffer what he suffered. *He* would take people in, he would provide the poor with meals and lodging, he would always be honest and kind — and that is exactly what he did.

As the saying goes, "Living well is the best revenge." And when someone hurts you, use your *yetzer hara*, use the desire for vengeance, and promise yourself that you'll show them just how great a human being can be.

Beside benefiting from these negative character traits which are the *Satan's* weaponry, it is sometimes possible to negotiate with the *yetzer hara* himself. A shopkeeper complained to Rav Meir Shapiro *z.l.* that he had no customers. Rav Shapiro advised him: When you are alone in the store, open a *sefer* and begin learning Torah. When the *Satan* sees you learning, he'll send customers; anything, just to keep you from the *mitzvah*.

The *sefarim* mention yet another way to negotiate with the *yetzer hara*, and that is to offer a compromise. For instance, if you decide you would like to stop screaming uncontrollably at your children, you might tell the *yetzer hara*: "Let's make a deal. After breakfast I will lose my temper totally, but not until breakfast is over." You are not really surrendering anything, because until now you have been blowing your top even before breakfast begins. But psychologically, once you officially decide, "I will not even *try* to be good the second hour," it becomes easier to work at improving the first. Try it! Unless the Satan feels so in charge that he has no need to negotiate, there is a chance of success; and from one successful hour you can move to the next.

Feelings of laziness and desires for physical pleasure are not so much traits of character as they are permanent parts of human nature. They must be dealt with on their own terms, and can sometimes be used for good. Lazy people do not get into arguments; they don't want to bother with all the hassle. Rav Nosson Tzvi Finkel of Slabodka also pointed out that some lazy people work very hard at their job, to be able to get it over with as quickly as possible. When you find yourself facing a mountain of work, a constructive use of laziness is to jump right in, so that you can return to the sofa without undue delay.

As for physical pleasure, we know that when our father Yitzchak decided to give his blessing to Eisav, he told Eisav to make him dinner. Some commentaries explain that Yitzchak knew Eisav was not so worthy to be blessed, and the father said: "At least let Eisav show respect by offering his father a good meal, and this will help me develop an enthusiasm to be able to bless him." It is like the *mitzvah* of *oneg Shabbos*, when even the holiest *tzaddik* is commanded to eat, to feel with his whole body the truth he already knows with his mind.

To take this down to our level, if there is a difficult *mitzvah* to be done — if you must clench your teeth at a PTA meeting or if you must carpool a load of armed and dangerous six-year-olds — then promise yourself a reward for doing it with a smile. If it's something pleasurable and legal — a food you enjoy, a good book — use it as an incentive. Besides helping you get the job done, it might also provide positive reinforcement that performing a *mitzvah* becomes associated in your mind with pleasurable things, and the pleasurable mental association eventually makes the *mitzvah* a pleasure in itself. (When you finish this chapter, don't forget to treat yourself to something nice.)

One more example of creatively using your *yetzer hara* is to spend time thinking about your eternal love of money.

Everyone loves money, and the Torah says that a judge who accepts a gift cannot remain impartial even if he so desires. After taking a penny, the judge can no longer see straight; that is the *yetzer's* power to use money to change over our whole way of thinking. Since it is so, why not use it to your advantage?

For instance, have you noticed that in recent years, long-distance operators have become more friendly? "How may I help you? Thank you for using AT&T!" Where did this sudden flowering of *mentchlichkeit* come from? The answer is that it came from Sprint, and MCI, and all other competing long-distance services. Having lost its monopoly, AT&T knows that to make money in a competitive market, one must be courteous to customers.

The trick is to realize that in some way, everyone you meet is your potential customer, and it will *pay* you to be friendly. If you are a salesman or a politician, you know this already. When I became a congregational rabbi I discovered that every Jew I met was a potential new member for the *shul* or someone I could marry, bury or sell *chametz* for.

Even if you don't work outside the home, you might someday want to sell your neighbors the idea of electing you president of the *yeshivah's* ladies' auxiliary, or the day may come when you will need to sell them a raffle ticket or some Tupperware. This is not a suggestion that all our relationships be transformed into money-making opportunities. But recognizing that cultivating friends and being cordial to everyone we meet is also in our own selfish best interest makes it a lot easier to be loving and cordial, even when we don't feel like it. If the idea helps, it's an idea to be used.

We could sum up everything in this chapter with the famous advice of the Gemara: One should always engage in studying Torah and performing *mitzvos* even for the wrong reasons, because the habit of doing good, once ingrained in us, will eventually bring us to do good for all the reasons that are right.

Take the case of someone who avoids arguments because of his *ga'avah*, his foolish pride which causes him to think it beneath his dignity to dispute with someone he considers his inferior. But if we get into the habit of *not* arguing, for any reason, after a while we begin to see that most issues people fight over truly are petty, and truly are beneath any decent person's human dignity, *ga'avah* or not.

Synagogues have been torn asunder by disputes over who should be given which *aliyah* to the Torah, and communities have experienced violence over questions of who should receive which honor or title or seat at the annual *yeshivah* dinner. If we can come to see the childishness of it all, how we are all being conned by the *yetzer hara* into wasting our lives over nothing, then we can hope to rise above pettiness, for the very best of reasons. With a clear perception of the truth, then even when we ourselves are the injured party, we can accept the situation and sometimes even laugh about it.

During a New York City garbage strike, one gentleman managed to have his trash collected daily without fail. Each morning he would place his garbage in a box, wrap it in colored paper and a ribbon, and leave it on the front seat of his car with the door unlocked and the window open. He would take a fifteen-minute walk, and when he returned he invariably found that his trash had been "collected."

That is a true story which is also a *mashal*, a parable for living. When we see how people develop ulcers over meaningless status symbols, how we often become enraged over imaginary slights and injustices, and how so much of our lives is such a great to-do about nothing, we begin to realize how funny it all is. You have to smile, as you let others fight over who should be the one to grab hold of the expensively wrapped package, which you know contains nothing but garbage with a ribbon on top. Using our vanity, our own personalized *yetzer hara*, to remain aloof from foolishness, can in the end enable us to recognize just how foolish the *yetzer hara* truly is.

Using your *yetzer hara* to defeat him is also an act of kindness to the *yetzer hara* himself. The *Aruch HaShulchan* writes that the *Satan's* great joy in life is to see you prevail over him; even *he* is rooting for you to succeed. Making proper use of the *yetzer hara* will perhaps also help us arouse the *yetzer hatov*, to allow us to come to perform *mitzvos, bechol levavcha,* with both *yetzers*; feeling love for Hashem and love for his children, giving us the *simchah* of true *hatzlachah* (success), and the *hatzlachah* of true *simchah*, in everything we do.

The Secret of Being Wicked

The *sefer Cheshbon HaNefesh* points out that even the most inspiring works of *mussar* are in themselves generally not sufficient to effect permanent changes in patterns of behavior. To modify lifelong habits and attitudes requires, in addition to inspiration, a practical plan, some step-by-step program for self-improvement.

What we need today is a handbook for people like ourselves, entitled, perhaps: "The Secret of Being Righteous; a Practical Guide to Becoming a *Tzaddik*." Unfortunately, such books are not readily available in stores, nor is this writer qualified to compose one himself.

However, in many areas of study, we can often learn something about our intellectual objective by examining its exact opposite. A police detective is trained to understand the *modus operandi* of criminals; a good used-car salesman learns what causes consumer resistance; and every first-year dental student is well versed in the causes of tooth decay. Therefore, in striving for self-improvement, perhaps a first step towards becoming a *tzaddik* is also to consider its opposite: How does one become a *rasha*? What is the secret of being truly wicked?

You may argue that it is no secret at all; doing bad things just comes naturally. Granted, some people do appear to be born with this ability — perhaps your boss, sometimes your relatives — but the matter is not so simple.

Our tradition is that over the centuries, as we travel in time further away from the experience of Mount Sinai, we have experienced a steady decline in spiritual power. In the time of *Tanach* we were blessed with literally thousands of prophets. When prophecy ceased, many *tzaddikim* still possessed the Divine inspiration of *ruach haKodesh*; but today, on the whole, we do not have access to *tzaddikim* such as those of the past.

However, Rav Nosson Tzvi Finkel of Slabodka pointed out that there is another side to this decline, which is: Just as the loss of spiritual power has cost us our great *tzaddikim*, so too, we no longer possess the greatest *resha'im*; outstanding wickedness is also more and more difficult to find.

This may be hard to believe, especially if you ride the New York City subway system. But our Sages tell us that in the days of the prophets there were wicked people who were Jews who recognized their Creator, who lived with complete faith in the power of Hashem; but who deliberately went out to fight Him, in rebellion against His authority. We don't see that sort of evil today, because spiritual power in general has become weaker in every respect. So let us begin our study of evil by going all the way back, to the first crime mentioned openly in the Torah.

The first sin was, of course, Adam and Eve eating from the

forbidden tree. Unfortunately, the contemporary moral decline leads most people today to view that sort of transgression as weakness rather than true evil, a surrender to temptation (compulsive-eating disorder?) rather than crime. The first major wickedness even moderns can identify with was the second sin recorded in the Torah, Adam's son Cain murdering his brother Abel. Each brother had brought a sacrificial offering to Hashem, only Abel's offering was accepted, and because of this Cain killed him.

Those of us who are blessed with siblings are aware that even if we are indeed sometimes envious of them, when was the last time any of us made a truly serious attempt to commit murder? Cain was a prophet! Hashem spoke directly to him. How does a prophet become transformed into a killer?

Ramban, in his commentary on *Chumash*, gives the answer: Cain was afraid. When Hashem accepted Abel's offering and not Cain's, Cain took it as a sign that Abel was permanently favored. Cain thought to himself: What will be the future? The world will be given to my brother and his children, and I and my descendants will be lost. In Cain's mind, Abel became a terrible threat; and one thought led to another, until he took a stone to smash in his brother's skull.

The secret of being wicked is fear. The Gemara tells us that if a small child is locked in a closet, we may desecrate the Shabbos to smash open the door to save him, even if the child has sufficient food and oxygen, because fear by itself is also dangerous. Human terror can lead to virtually anything: death from shock, or suicide, or even murder.

Yaakov's brother Eisav was one of the great villains of history. He tried to kill Yaakov, the apparent reason being the blessings Yaakov had received from their father. But in the end, after Eisav finally made peace with Yaakov, Eisav moved away; the land was not big enough for both of them. The Torah says that Eisav went *because of Yaakov*, or *from the face of Yaakov* (*Genesis* 36:6). He left to get away from his brother's face, the Midrash says, because Eisav, with all his physical strength and men-at-arms, was afraid.

What was the fear? Eisav measured himself against his righteous brother, and he could not compete. Instead of defining himself in terms of his own potential and working to develop it, Eisav made his entire self-esteem dependent upon the comparison; inevitably, that made Yaakov a threat. First, Eisav tried to kill him, and later, after making peace, Eisav had to flee.

Going further in our history, the beginnings of organized anti-Semitism were in Egypt, when Pharaoh and his people enslaved us. The righteous Yosef had been a national hero who saved Egypt from famine, and the children of Israel were living peaceably as loyal citizens. What caused the change in Egyptian attitudes? The Torah tells us that the Egyptian king said (*Shemos* 1:9,10): *The nation of the children of Israel are more numerous, and more powerful than us . . . If war breaks out, it* (Israel) *will join our enemies and attack us.*

Our ancestors had no desire to harm Egypt. If anything, the Midrash says, the Israelites were busy assimilating, becoming more Egyptian than the Egyptians themselves. But that is the power of paranoia, the horrible effects of Pharaoh's fear.

When we finally left Egypt, traveling to *Eretz Yisrael*, we had no quarrel with the neighboring people of Moav or with King Sichon the Emorite. But the Torah says that *Moav was afraid* (*Numbers* 22:3). They thought we would attack them, and they hired the sorcerer Bilam to destroy us first. When Moshe Rabbeinu asked King Sichon for permission to pass through his land, had Sichon consented we would have gone through in peace, and had he refused we would have detoured around him. Instead, he came out to war against us.

You might wonder, if these nations were truly afraid, why are they blamed for their sins? But it seems clear that the source of their fear was that they projected their own wickedness onto Israel. Pharaoh, Moav and Sichon all thought: "If we were more powerful than the next people, surely we would conquer them. Should we believe that Moshe is more righteous than us?" That wickedness was the sin.

The Sages add that anti-Semitism throughout history is also

based on a certain fear. Hashem offered the Torah to all peoples, but they refused to accept the awesome responsibility; when Israel accepted the Torah, we showed it could be done. As the Gemara puts it, the name Mount Sinai comes from the word *sinah*, hatred, because truth produces hate in those who refuse to see it. As the French philosopher Pascal wrote, a man who is forced to confront his failure develops a mortal hatred against that truth which shows him his faults.

If we are afraid, if we are lacking in trust, we can transform best friends into enemies. Many parents do this to their children, and husbands and wives to each other: The suspicion and lack of confidence in the other person become the cause which pushes the other person away, and our fear of losing their love is what destroys the love. In *Tanach*, the king of Amon befriended King David; and when the king died, David sent a delegation to console and honor his son. But the Amonites' suspicious reaction was to assume that David's messengers must be spies, which led to war and Amon's own downfall.

This insanity affects relations between non-Jewish nations as well. For example, the South seceded from the United States in 1861 because they feared that Congress might interfere with the spread of slavery. Their overreaction led to the Civil War, and the total abolition of slavery in the South itself. Forty years later, Kaiser Wilhelm of Germany suspected that England and France were plotting against him. They were not, at the time. But the Kaiser, with public accusations and threats, single-handedly caused England and France to form an alliance, in order to protect themselves against him.

In 1916, Irish rebels started their "Easter Rebellion" against England, which was quickly crushed. This was during World War I, and most Irishmen supported England. As the rebels were dragged through the streets of Dublin, the Irish populace booed them as traitors. However, England, being afraid, ordered mass reprisals; and the British government in one stroke caused all Ireland to turn against them, leading to Irish independence.

This principle is well established, in both *Tanach* and general history. What is not so well established is that it also applies to each of *us*.

When we are angry with someone, often it is not so much what the other person did, as it is the perceived threat to our own self-image. If I feel secure in myself, another person's insults or even outright treachery does not eat me up inside. I may have to react, but I do not have to lose sleep or my health. However, if I am not secure in myself, then I end up using other people's opinions of me as my validation, the yardstick to measure my soul. The need of other people's approval creates a chronic fear, which leads to chronic pain, without relief.

The ethical classic *Mesillas Yesharim* teaches that fear takes over the imagination, and causes us to create problems that do not exist. It is human to rationalize, and we can end up creating entire philosophies out of nothing. After King Shlomo died, Israel was divided between ten tribes in the north and two in the south. The North was more powerful, but the South had Jerusalem and the *Beis HaMikdash.*

King Yeravam of the North said to himself: "On *Yom Tov*, when we all visit the *Beis HaMikdash,* I will be just another guest in this holy place that belongs to my competitor, the king of the South. Perhaps my own people will abandon me!" Because of this, Yeravam created a new ideology: He proclaimed that Hashem does not want us to go to the wicked Jersualem, not even to the *Mikdash*. To make certain no one went, Yeravam set up guards at the border, and he ended up constructing his own Temple, complete with golden calves.

Yeravam was not a charlatan. It appears that he came to believe his own propaganda, because a man who is afraid is willing to bend truth into pretzels, if it will lead to a real or imaginary path of escape.

And therefore, whenever we are faced with someone who is angry or complaining, we should always ask: What is *really* disturbing them? The problem may be quite different from what they say it is. And also when we ourselves are upset, we should confront ourselves to honestly examine the cause of our pain. Is it indeed because of some new specific problem? Or is it because the problem is arousing some hidden anxiety, a terror that lies buried deep inside ourselves?

Thus far we have been focusing on fear as an impediment to performance of *mitzvos* between fellow humans. What about *mitzvos* directly between a human being and his Creator? In *kashrus*, Shabbos or Torah study, is fear part of the "secret of being wicked" in those *mitzvos* as well?

The first sin mentioned in the Torah was Adam and Eve eating the forbidden fruit, something of a *kashrus*-related problem. The serpent who enticed them was not your common rattlesnake or python. From the Midrash and later commentators we see that this serpent represents the enticement of evil, the powerful forces that lead people to do wrong.

The first humans had been commanded to refrain from partaking of the fruit of this one tree, nothing more. Along comes the serpent to say: *Indeed, has the Lord forbidden you all the trees of the garden!* (Genesis 3:1). It was like a child who complains: "Mommy, you never give me anything!" Adults work the same way, and the little voice inside is whining: "If you follow the Torah, you won't have any fun at all."

The serpent continued its sales pitch: The real reason Hashem prohibited this tree is: *Hashem knows that if you eat this one fruit, you yourselves will become Divine* (Genesis 3:5). That means: "If you give up this one pleasure, you will lose *everything*. You *must* have it." Those are two voices of enticement to go against the Torah, voices we hear inside ourselves daily: "If I keep the *mitzvah*, I'll have nothing; if I transgress, then I'll have everything." And aren't those voices also expressions of fear?

There was a Jew who abandoned his wife and children after more than twenty years of marriage. He was not Jewishly observant, but his rabbi called him to ask why he was leaving his family. He replied: "I care about my wife, and I love my children. But rabbi, I'm already fifty years old. This is my last chance!"

Last chance for what? Sadly, this man had gone through life

believing that he had lost all happiness by not being a swinging single. And now, in his second half-century, he will find his happiness?

Those who are familiar with the singles scene know full well that it is not the Shangri-la of contentment. But this man was so afraid of missing out on this imagined bliss that he threw away his family for a mirage. As Rav Yisrael Salanter was wont to say: "A man trades his whole life for a toy whistle; and then in the end, he discovers the whistle doesn't even work."

Another kind of fear which prevents us from doing *mitzvos* is fear of being ridiculed. The *Mesillas Yesharim* writes that someone who is fully convinced of what is right may still do wrong, because he is terrified of being different from his friends.

On Shabbos, unnecessary exertion is forbidden, and it is generally forbidden for adults to run. One of the Sages of the Gemara said: "When I saw the Rabbis running to the Torah lecture, I used to say, 'They are desecrating the Shabbos!' But now that I have heard the *halachah* that one should always run to do *mitzvos*, even on Shabbos, now I also run." The question is: Why did the Sage have to add that now that he knows the *halachah*, he also runs? Of course he runs! Once he knows it is a *mitzvah*, certainly the Sages performed all the *mitzvos*! And perhaps it means:

Although he himself had formerly believed that running on Shabbos is always forbidden, and even though he used to publicly criticize others for running, still, once he found that they were right and he was wrong, he was not ashamed to start running himself, even at the risk of some smirks and I-told-you-sos. The fear of embarrassment is so difficult to overcome that doing so is a heroism worth recording in the Gemara, for all of us to follow.

This fear that compels us not to be different from our neighbors can also hold us back from improving in any way that makes us different from our own previous selves. One reason why older people are less open to change in general is that they have an emotional investment in a particular life style. Changing implies an admission that up till now they may have been wrong, a fearful admission for most people to make.

I was acquainted with a *shomer Shabbos* family in Brooklyn whose two sons attended Jewish day-schools. After the older son completed the eighth grade, his father sent him to public high school to "broaden his horizons." Tragically, after two years, the boy had been so ruined that he was hardly recognizable as Jewish. Then the younger son graduated from the eighth grade, a sweet, innocent child, and the father once again had to decide: Jewish school or public school?

He had all the evidence of his older son in front of his nose. But for the father to admit his mistake would be tantamount to confessing that he had spiritually murdered his own son. He would not confess that crime, not even to himself. So he concluded that the ruination of his older boy was a fluke, a freak accident, and he chose to send the younger boy to the same public high school.

A *Chumash* class at our local synagogue was faithfully attended by a certain student who came every week without fail, and then suddenly dropped out. When he was called to ask why, he replied: "I'm sorry, rabbi, but as you know, I'm not observant. And if I keep learning Torah, it is inevitable; I will have to *become* observant. So, I had to drop out." A success story! Learning Torah had convinced him of the Torah's truth — so he *stopped* learning, because he was afraid to face what he himself knew to be the truth. It is astonishing: How could he abandon the reality he himself believed in? But fear makes a Jew into an ostrich; stick your head in the sand, and maybe reality will go away.

There are men who would keep Shabbos, but are afraid it will harm their careers; married women who would cover their hair, but are afraid their "friends" will look down their noses at them; parents who would push their children to do the right thing, but are afraid the child won't "like" them anymore. And there are thousands of Jews who are interested in coming to a *shul* or a *shiur*, but they worry that one *mitzvah* will lead to another, and who knows what might happen?

That is why it was written in the *sefer Minchas Shmuel,* almost two hundred years ago: To succeed, what a Jew needs most of all is *bitachon*, a trust in Hashem; a faith to carry us over all the obstacles of which we are so afraid.

Let us consider a possible objection to everything written above. If it is true that fear is the major obstacle, and if this is indeed a key point to act on in the process of *teshuvah* and self-improvement, why then is it not mentioned in our *davening*? Our *tefillos* speak so much about sin and repentance, especially at Rosh Hashanah; why do they not at least touch upon this major problem of being afraid?

The answer is: The prayers *do* mention it. During the season of repentance we repeat those prayers, not once or twice, but over a hundred times. From the beginning of Elul to the end of Succos, twice daily we proclaim: *A song of David: Hashem is my light and my salvation, from whom shall I be afraid? Hashem is the strength of my life, from whom shall I tremble?* (Psalm 27:1). That entire chapter is King David confronting human fear, his and ours.

He speaks of enemies. And he speaks of the fear of loneliness: *For my father and mother have left me* (ibid. v.10). And he speaks of the fear of the journey after death: *If not for my faith that I will see the Divine goodness in the land of eternal life . . .* (ibid. v.13). We begin the month of Elul with this prayer, and it accompanies us morning and evening throughout the process of *teshuvah* and forgiveness.

And now that we know the secret of being wicked, how can we use the information for good? How do we deal with our anxieties, day by day? A first step is to admit that anxieties exist. The refusal to face problems only makes them worse.

The matador Juan Belmonte was famed for his nerves of steel. He would often kneel in the bull ring, inches from the bull's nose. When the bull charged, he would not sidestep, but instead used his cape to maneuver the bull out of his way. But Belmonte, who was so extraordinarily brave (or foolhardy), suffered from a nervous stutter! Similarly, there was an American soldier in World War II who was decorated for heroism in risking his life under enemy fire, but was terrified to go to the dentist! The reason for this anomaly is that even courageous people have certain fears in life, which are perfectly normal. But those who are ashamed of their fears push them under a mental rug, not to admit their existence, which only make the fears grow even larger. Bringing worries out in the open will enable us to examine them under the light and deal with them.

In getting along with others, we should not assume that people are completely rational, because virtually no one is. Every person has hidden worries, fears stretching all the way back to childhood; fears which create unknown tensions, and which make many people liable to explode at anytime.

This does not mean that people are bad. But with all their goodness, they must be handled by us with kid gloves: to be as sensitive as we can, and to show with a smile that we care; because, in some way, each of us looks to the other to tell him not to be afraid. As the prophet says: *Tell your brother, be strong!* (*Isaiah* 41:6). "Telling him" is part of our life's work, with every brother and sister we meet.

In dealing with fears of our own, a most useful tool is a saying of the Gerrer Rebbi, Reb Itche Meir *z.l.*: "Fear of anything other than Hashem is *avodah zarah,* idolatry. To fear something is to worship that thing, and worship may be offered only to Hashem."

How does one overcome an attraction to idol worship? Logical argument is helpful, to point out the idol's foolishness. But in addition to logic, the Gemara says: "All mockery is forbidden, except for mockery of idol worship." Making fun of it and degrading it are the ways to overcome its irrational temptation. (Is this the underlying reason why there are so many Jewish comedians, talented people, who unfortunately do not know how to direct their talent to its spiritual end?)

Fear is *avodah zarah*. And therefore, one way to overcome fear is to train oneself to learn to laugh at it. A simple technique is to take a foolish fear and exaggerate it. Occasionally, I serve on committees requiring me to make telephone calls soliciting funds for *tzedakah*. I often hesitate to make the call (most of us are shy about asking other people for their money); so I tell myself:

"You are afraid to call, aren't you? Yes indeed, because you know what terrible thing might happen. If you ask him to give *tzedakah*, he might *refuse*! Not only might he refuse, but he might even tell everyone, Miller had the *chutzpah* to call him for money! He will put ads in the local newspaper, he'll picket my home, television talk-show hosts will come down, and the entire civilized world will point their fingers in shame and say: the scandal of Watergate, Televangelists, Savings and Loans fraud, and now, Miller telephoning people to solicit *tzedakah*." By that time, if I can control my own laughter, I make the call.

When we hesitate to perform a *mitzvah* out of fear of ridicule, we must recognize that this is indeed permitting the other person to become a deity over us. Why should we allow neighbors or relatives or Paris fashion designers to determine our personal religious and moral standards?

For example: If you desire to upgrade certain personal *mitzvah* standards, but you worry about possible negative reactions from your sister-in-law, what do you do? In your mind, try to imagine her as the Queen from Alice in Wonderland. She has an enormous crown, a baby face, and she goes around yelling, "Off with your head!" (You can also add a baby rattle in one hand and a pacifier in the other.) The idea is not to degrade your relatives; but if you are indeed afraid of them, that imaginary ogre should be inflated in your mind until the bubble finally bursts.

In a sense, *avodah zarah*, idolatry, can apply also to oneself. If we hesitate to explore a new *mitzvah* because it differs from what we have always done in the past, and we do not want to admit that we may have been wrong until now, that is auto-idolatry: "I'm a deity, I'm perfect, how can I have been mistaken until now?"

People persist in this stubbornness not so much from arrogance as from a fear that admitting error means admitting they are stupid or worthless; but that is a misconception of what it means to be a human being. When Thomas Edison invented the electric light bulb, the only way to discover a filament was to test different materials one by one. He went through literally thousands of failures until he discovered tungsten. Was Edison a failure, because his experiments to create an electric light bulb failed literally thousands of times and succeeded only once? Trial and error is the nature of research, and the work is judged by the final breakthrough.

A Jew is also engaged in research: the study of the science of living a life of virtue and true success. To succeed, we must have experience, through trial and error; and even with the Torah's guidance, we will all end up making thousands of choices that do not work well and need to be altered. Don't call them mistakes. They are experiments; and each day we perform more of them, discovering more and more the behavior patterns that do work, if we are only willing to try — more Torah learning, a new area of attention to a *mitzvah* or a trait of good character. Try it out in your own life's laboratory, and discover where the *kedushah* will take you.

At the risk of writing something which may sound outrageous, can we suggest that there are some observant Jews who engage in idolatry by confusing an *avodah zarah* with Hashem? Meaning: If, in our loyalty to the Creator, we have a totally erroneous conception of Who the Creator is; if one serves Hashem but believes that Hashem has a physical body, *chas veshalom*, surely that is also *avodah zarah*.

But does this idea apply to us? Perhaps.

We know that *yiras Shamayim*, the fear of Hashem, is a *mitzvah*. It is a healthy fear, the awe of standing before infinite greatness and love, and knowing that this Supreme Being cares for you, every moment, forever. But there are sincere people who fear Hashem in the wrong way, a fear that can lead them to spiritual collapse.

King David said in *Tehillim*: *Hashem, You are the One Who forgives, in order that You may be feared* (Psalms 130:4). The *Ramban* explains: People tell themselves that, having sinned, they are now irredeemably lost. "I've done wrong for years, I'm

The Secret of Being Wicked □ 85

just no good. And since I'm lost anyway, I might as well forget about Torah entirely." That fear of worthlessness and hopelessness is *avodah zarah*, because that picture of a Father in Heaven Who gives up on you is totally false.

Hashem creates every person *b'tzelem Elokim,* in the Divine image, with a spark of sanctity that refuses to be extinguished. All of us can improve, no one is irretrievably lost, and our Father always stands ready to take us back. "You are the One Who forgives"; because if You did not forgive, we would abandon You in despair. But because You *do* forgive, we always have another chance, and we are encouraged not to give up, but to fight to return to You and to hold You in awe, day by day.

It happened in the *shul* of the Kotzker *z.l.*, that in the middle of *davening* his *shammas* banged on the *bimah* and said: "The Rebbe has told me to announce to everyone, that indeed, there *is* a *Ribono Shel Olam."* It means: Hashem does not merely exist. He *is*. He is here, with us, listening; and ready to help. Another famous saying of the Kotzker is: "Where is Hashem? Wherever we permit Him to enter."

By inviting Him into our lives, and asking Him to stay, we can ourselves echo the words of *Tehillim*. And then we will know the secret of how to vanquish all our fears and to conclude, as David did: *Await Hashem's aid, strengthen and fortify your heart, and await Hashem (Psalms* 27:14)), for He will arrive — if you let Him.

Who Needs You?

In studying Torah, there is a level of sophistication at which one comes to recognize that certain activities can be considered a *mitzvah* for one person, and an *aveirah*, a sin, for someone else. The Gemara tells of a man who came to town dressed in mourning. When asked what tragedy had occurred, he replied that he was mourning the destruction of the *Beis HaMikdash* and Jerusalem. A *mitzvah*! The reaction of the local Sages was: Put him in jail.

Meaning, we all should feel for the destruction of the *Beis HaMikdash*, but for an ordinary person to display public mourning, except on Tishah B'Av, may be mere exhibitionism and false piety. So, whether or not a particular act is a *mitzvah* may depend on the time, if it's Tishah B'Av or not, and on the person, whether he is a known *tzaddik* or not.

Similarly, in the Rosh Hashanah and Yom Kippur *davening*, it would appear self-evident that we should concentrate on asking for another year of life. Hashem has before Him the Books of Life and Death, and one would certainly expect the whole thrust of our prayers to be: *HaKadosh Baruch Hu*, save us! Let us live another year!

Nonetheless, the most important prayer in the *machzor*, the silent *Shemoneh Esrei*, says very little about staying alive: A line or two at the beginning, *zachreinu l'chaim* (remember us for life), and near the end, *uchesov l'chaim tovim* (inscribe us for a good life); but the entire middle of the main body of the *Shemoneh Esrei* does not speak of life at all. Commentaries tell us that even *zachreinu l'chaim* and *uchesov l'chaim* were not part of the original *Shemoneh Esrei* but were added at a later date.

What then do we ask for? "Hashem, may Your Name be sanctified in the world." "May everyone revere You," and may they all unite to serve You, and may You give honor to the righteous and remove all evil and all should see that You are sole King of the Universe. Those are beautiful ideals; but my *life* is on the line! Who has time to talk about sanctifying Hashem's Name in the world when I should be asking to save my own skin?

The *sefer Yesod VeShoresh HaAvodah* explains that on Rosh Hashanah and Yom Kippur, just as there is judgment on our lives, so too is it judged whether the glory of Hashem will be revealed in the year to come. Billions of people do not recognize Hashem, and that is a disgrace to the honor *HaKadosh Baruch Hu* should receive. So the *Yesod VeShoresh HaAvodah* says: Yes, you are now being judged on your own life or death, but don't be selfish. Instead of praying for your life, pray for something more important, that Divine honor should increase in the world. You may die? Granted that's a problem, but the main thing is to pray for *kiddush Hashem*, that more people should recognize the truth. It is for this reason that the *Shemoneh Esrei's* main theme is not personal need but Divine glory, because that is what truly counts.

That is the writing of an old-time *tzaddik*, a spiritual giant telling us to forget ourselves and think only of Hashem. And you might think, "That's what I'll do; I won't concentrate on asking for life, I'll just think about *kavod Shamayim*, Divine glory, that is the *mitzvah*."

Then along came Rav Yisrael Salanter to tell us *not* to think that way. For a *tzaddik* who devotes his entire life to Hashem, it makes sense that on Rosh Hashanah he prays only for his Creator's honor. But for the rest of us, for people who spend twenty-three hours and fifty-nine minutes a day thinking about ourselves, to stand up on Rosh Hashanah and say, "I won't think of my life, I'll think only of Hashem," is not a *mitzvah* of self-sacrifice. It is merely an indication that we never had a feeling for the Day of Judgment in the first place.

If I knew that today my life is truly at stake, I would not be thinking about Divine honor. I couldn't. If a car is racing towards me at 60 mph I don't consider whether it is in keeping with the honor of Torah for me to run in the street — I jump out of the way. Rav Yisrael Salanter therefore said that nowadays, the correct way to perform the *mitzvah* is *not* to place our emphasis on the billions of non-Jews who don't honor Hashem. Instead, if you feel the holiness of the day, you will be thinking, "Write us down for another year of life."

So we have two different approaches, depending on who you are: (1) Great *tzaddikim* should pray for an increase in *HaKadosh Baruch Hu's* glory. (2) Ordinary folks should concentrate on asking to remain living. But we can ask: Since most people are not great *tzaddikim* and should be focusing on *davening* for their lives, why then did the Sages who composed the *Shemoneh Esrei* not put the emphasis on life? The *Shemoneh Esrei* was composed by rabbis and prophets over two thousand years ago, a prayer formulated for all Jews for all time, including Jews like us. Since our concern should be to request life, why do we have a prayer whose entire theme is: Lord, rule the world and glorify Your Name?

On Rosh Hashanah we are judged for the coming year, based on how we have spent the year gone by. When a great *tzaddik's* record comes before the Heavenly court, it sees all his thousands of vibrant *mitzvos*, and several shriveled-up sins of which the *tzaddik* has already repented, and he is judged favorably. But for many of us, if *we* appear before the court with our piles of sins and our half-hearted *mitzvos* and we ask for life, the Divine response might be: What for? I've given you so many years of life until now, why should I throw away good money after bad? As a student once said to a philosopher, "I must live!"; to which the philosopher replied, "I do not perceive the necessity." So what are we to do if, based on our past season's batting average, the most logical decision is for *HaKadosh Baruch Hu* to drop us from the team?

In the United States Army, for an officer to succeed and be promoted in rank, it is axiomatic that the accepted rules must be strictly obeyed. Orders must be followed and standards of military propriety upheld, or one's career is surely doomed.

In 1862, during the American Civil War, a Union Army officer named Ulysses S. Grant was ordered to attack a Confederate outpost adjacent to Fort Donelson, a southern fortress. He succeeded in capturing the outpost, and then said to himself: "While I'm here, why not capture the fortress also?" So he took his men, attacked Fort Donelson, and won the first major Union victory in the Civil War. As you can imagine, Grant's commanding officers were furious, because Grant had captured the fortress without orders to do so; he had broken the rules! Grant also had a reputation for drunkenness, and his critics were clamoring to get rid of him, but President Abraham Lincoln would not allow it. As he told one of the staff officers: "General, I can't spare this man — he *fights.*" He breaks the rules, he should be court-martialed; perhaps. But we can't think about that now, because we need him. He drinks? Lincoln said: "Find out what brand of whiskey he uses, and send bottles to all our other generals."

When someone is needed, other considerations are set aside.

On Rosh Hashanah and Yom Kippur we could pray for ourselves, and to some extent we do; but we've broken too many rules to expect an answer on that account. Instead, we ask Hashem: May You reign over the world; may all the world unite to serve You; and make evil vanish, and You be recognized as King. In page after page, the underlying theme is: Hashem, we're not so good, but we want to honor You, we want righteousness and sanctity to rule, we're on Your side; and after all, who else do You have? For we are Your children, Your servants, Your congregation, Your inheritance, Your sheep, Your vineyard, Your work, Your beloved, Your treasure and the ones You have exalted. Hashem, we don't *deserve* anything; but our presence on earth means *something,* we have a mission, we are needed.

This theme is repeated many times in the Torah: Individuals may not be worthy in themselves, but they have one *mitzvah*, one involvement with Torah or the Torah nation which makes them indispensable. And because the Master of the World "needs" them in His plan, so to speak, they are granted all kinds of undeserved blessings from Heaven.

The most important preparation for days of judgment is to do *teshuvah,* to repent and try to become true *tzaddikim.* But in addition to striving for that goal, it is a practical plan to look for ways in which we can become needed, for *mitzvos* and relationships which will cause the Heavenly court to say: "Even if they don't deserve it, we can't get rid of them so quickly."

Let's look at some examples:

Parashas Ha'azinu tells us: *For all His ways are justice . . . righteous and upright is He* (Deuteronomy 32:4). What does it mean that Hashem is the righteous judge; can't anyone else judge righteously?

One famous answer is: When a judge sentences a criminal, he tries to take into account the circumstances of the case, but he cannot possibly take into account all the ramifications of the sentence itself. If the criminal is sent to prison, his wife suffers, his children suffer, and his landlord and employer may also suffer. Also his grocer, baker, doctor, dentist, paperboy and everyone who had him as a customer or an acquaintance all lose because of it, but what can you do? However, Hashem is different. He sees all, and takes every effect into account, and He will not punish any one individual unless all those who also suffer deserve their share of anguish as well.

That is one factor in the decision whether to purchase life insurance. Imagine a fellow flying his private airplane, and at 5,000 feet he develops engine trouble. Angels in heaven assemble at the Heavenly court, and the prosecuting angel begins listing all the man's sins, suggesting that a plane crash would not be undeserving. The defending angels rush forward with all the fellow's *mitzvos*, but they're not enough. If only he had answered *amen* in *shul* a few more times . . . It looks bad for the defense, but they have one more argument. "Granted," they say, "this man deserves to go, but what about his poor wife and children; do they deserve to suffer? Shouldn't we save this Jew for their sake?" In reply, the prosecuting angel pulls out the man's $600,000 life-insurance policy. "He's insured, you needn't worry about the family quite so much," and the plane drops . . . For that reason, some Jews are wary about life insurance.

Whether to buy insurance is a halachic question, to be asked of the proper authorities. But the practical lesson for us right now is that before Rosh Hashanah, it pays to make as many friends as you can, so that there should be literally hundreds of people who don't want to see you go. There should be shopkeepers who want you because you're a polite customer, employers who need you because you're honest, neighbors who would be saddened to lose the smiles you share, charity organizations who would sorely miss the checks you send, and Torah teachers who don't want to lose you as a regular at the class or *shiur*. The more friends you have and the more people there are who would be saddened to lose you, the better your chances that Heaven will decide: Even if *he* doesn't deserve another year, it's too much to make all those other people suffer.

That's one way to make yourself indispensable, by making friends, so that doing away with you will be more trouble than it's worth. A second method is to find some worthy organization or institution, and become a necessary cog in its machinery. If your *shul* has difficulty getting a *minyan* in the morning and you're the tenth man, Hashem may decide that, even with all your sins, it is worth keeping you around. Or, have you noticed the elderly women who stand on street corners collecting for *tzedakah* institutions? There is a shortage of *tzedakah* collectors, and you can rest assured that *HaKadosh Baruch Hu* is in no hurry to order their demise.

On the subject of *tzedakah*, one of the all-time champion fundraisers and builders of Torah was the Ponovezher Rav *z.l.,* who founded the Ponovezh *Yeshivah* and many other Torah institutions in *Eretz Yisrael*. It happened that the Rav once had an ailment in his legs that prevent him from walking, and the great *Gaon*, the Chazon Ish *z.l.,* assured him that he would recover, which he did. How did the Chazon Ish know the illness was only temporary? Did he possess supernatural knowledge of *ruach haKodesh?* Well, undoubtedly he did; but besides *ruach haKodesh,* the Chazon Ish explained that, although you can't expect to live forever, since the core of the Rav's existence was traveling for his *yeshivah*, Hashem would not keep him alive while taking away his mobility; that could not be.

I do not know how far the Chazon Ish's assurance extends (perhaps you have to be a Ponovezher Rav to receive it). But there are so many Torah institutions which are suffering from an underabundance of volunteers, that if we join one — fundraising, *shul* activities, *shiurim, chesed* projects — it gives each of us the merit of being truly needed. The same is true when we work at raising a loyal Jewish family. If you are caring for children who need you, and you are helping them to become healthy, happy, Torah-committed Jews, then you are working on a vital project, and the angels will think twice before suggesting that you be fired.

(There is of course no *mitzvah* with which we may *demand* another year of life, and no merit which guarantees that all our wishes will be fulfilled. Jews perform *mitzvos* from pure loyalty, and Hashem grants life from pure *chesed*. Nevertheless, the Torah lesson that indispensable people have special merit is there to teach us that this is the path for us to take, together with *tefillos* acknowledging that all blessings are only acts of Divine grace.)

There is also a third way to be needed, which is less well known. A *Kohen* is not permitted to come in contact with a dead body, and a *Kohen Gadol*, a High Priest, does not even attend the funeral of his parents. But there is one case where a *Kohen* and *Kohen Gadol* are permitted and even obligated to participate in a burial, and that is if a Jew dies and there is no one else to bury him; that's how important a *mes mitzvah* is.

Almost a thousand years ago, the great Rav Yehudah HaChassid wrote that although all *mitzvos* are eternally valuable, one which is especially precious is any *mitzvah* that other people tend to ignore. If there is a mitzvah nobody wants, Rav Yehudah calls it a *mes mitzvah,* like a Jew who has no one to bury him. If you are the one to take up the cause of that *mitzvah* and fulfill it, you now have the *mitzvah* on your side as your patron. And even if in general you are not so worthy, still, you are the one upholding the honor of this particular *mitzvah* in your neighborhood; and Heaven may well be inclined to let you off easy, because the Torah itself needs you.

To find a *mitzvah* that not too many people are keeping is easy, and we could almost go through the *Shulchan Aruch* picking out *halachos* at random. But as an example, let us choose one particular *mitzvah* which includes many details, and which many Jews have never even heard of.

Parashas Kedoshim commands us, *Sanctify yourselves* (*Leviticus* 19:2). The *Ramban's* commentary explains this by saying that in virtually every *mitzvah* a loophole can be found if one looks hard enough, and by using the loophole one can destroy the entire spirit of the *mitzvah*. We can observe all the laws of Shabbos, and still not use it as a day of rest and spiritual regeneration. We can be technically honest in business, and use every law in the book to cheat the other fellow. We can keep 100% kosher, and still eat like wild savages. Therefore, the *Ramban* writes, the Torah gives many general moral imperatives, commanding us not to try to escape through loopholes: (1) When partaking of physical pleasure, be holy. (2) Besides observing the *laws* of Shabbos, make it a true day of rest. (3) Aside from refraining from stealing, make sure to do what is right and good.

That is a general Torah principle, not to try to avoid a *mitzvah* and it is a principle that is so overlooked, that if you adopt it — even in just one area — you will have a *mes mitzvah* of your very own, a *mitzvah* which makes you a wanted man, or woman, in the eyes of Hashem.

For instance, we all know, *Thou shall not steal* (*Exodus* 20:13). But when I purchased airline tickets from my friendly neighborhood travel agent, she said: "Rabbi, your two-year-old, how tall is she? If she's little, you can take her for free, if you don't tell the airline that she's already two." I said to the agent: "But she *is* two, and I'm not a crook." "Yes, but they don't ask at the plane, and they'll never know."

I finally managed to convince the lady that despite her good intentions, I wanted to pay for the ticket, and she sold it to me. Now, what is the *halachah*? According to the law of the Torah, may you take a two-year-old on a plane without paying, or a short six-year-old (five is the cutoff year in our town) on a bus? The answer, of course, is that you should ask your local rabbi. But even if it would be permitted to "get away with it," wouldn't this be a beautiful *mitzvah* to adopt as your own, to be extra-strict at honesty? Not to make long-distance person-to-person telephone calls to yourself, and not to keep extra change when the storekeeper accidentally gives you more than you deserve, and not to ask auto mechanics or medical technicians to inflate bills to fool insurance companies. Whether or not the law is that you *have* to do so, at the very least, you will be adopting a lonely *mitzvah*, a *mitzvah* that needs you.

Another example: The *halachah* is very clear that conversation in *shul* is permitted only if it is necessary for *davening*, a *mitzvah*, or words of Torah. So where does the practice of talking sports and politics in *shul* come from? Torah authorities express surprise at the blatant disregard of this *halachah*, and some suggest that perhaps there are *some* grounds for leniency to permit *some* of the conversations that take place in our synagogues today. Perhaps. But even if you think such talk is permissible, wouldn't it be a unique contribution to the Jewish community in your neighborhood if there was a Jew who decided that he or she is not going to talk to anyone in *shul* except *HaKadosh Baruch Hu?* You can be polite, but when your friend asks you about the Mets or the Dodgers, take him outside to answer. It's an original *mitzvah* for you to perform, and in many *shuls* you'll have virtually no competition.

In *mitzvos* like *kashrus* and Shabbos it is often more difficult to find loopholes in the law, so many people become Jewish constitutional lawyers and say: Everything is innocent until proven guilty, everything is permitted until proven otherwise. There are observant Jews who eat foods of questionable *kashrus* without checking, and Jews who place food on the stove on Shabbos, "since no one ever told me I can't, it's probably o.k." Those aren't really loopholes at all. But if you wish to possess a *mitzvah* of your very own, why not make it a project to research one area of *halachah*, to learn how to do it exactly right? Wouldn't it be wonderful if people would say: "Cooking on Shabbos? (Your name) is the expert. *Kashrus?* Watch what (your name) does in the kitchen."

One last example, which is the most famous loophole of them all: The Torah prohibition against *lashon hara*, slanderous talk, is accepted by all Jews. Even Reform clergy have not abolished it, nor have the Conservatives modified it, and there is no argument between left and right wings of Orthodoxy that this *mitzvah* is something for all of us to keep. So how come so many people still don't keep it?

One obvious reason is that gossip is fun. Every week, millions of supermarket shoppers pay good money to buy tabloid newspaper / scandal sheets to find out what brand of diapers Princess so-and-so uses, or which show-business celebrity is getting married or divorced. Foolish or not, it's *geshmak*.

But another reason why people speak *lashon hara* is that there are certain exceptional cases where it is permitted. If someone is planning to invest in a disastrous business-partnership or a disastrous marriage, it's a *mitzvah* to warn them of the dangers, if they'll listen. But because of these exceptions, people tend to say, "Well, *this* is not real *lashon hara,* or, it's important for people to know, or, it's a *mitzvah* to talk about that guy," etc.

We should learn what it is that the Torah permits and prohibits, but there's another approach which for many people is more practical: Why not make it your own personal *mitzvah* not to speak badly about others, even when it's technically permitted? Except to save another from actual harm, resolve not to slander acquaintances, in-laws, institutions, large groups of Jews, or even Rabbis.

Let's not argue whether it is permitted to talk about them. Let's even pretend it might be allowed to speak negatively about neighbors, Israelis, or Russian Jews (and everyone knows you're allowed to speak about Rabbis, both local and international). But even so, if someone would adopt as their personal *mitzvah* not to speak badly about anyone, that there should be at least one Jew on the block who never slanders anybody; wouldn't that be a *mes mitzvah,* an altruistic achievement to be a source of enormous pride? As the Chofetz Chaim said: In the old days, there were so many great *tzaddikim* around that the average person didn't have much chance. But today, with so little competition, even a small effort can make you outstanding in the spiritual field of your choice.

And if we can succeed in making ourselves truly needed by friends, *shuls*, *yeshivos* and organizations, and by *mitzvos* which are not greatly in demand, then we can hope for a Heavenly decree of a good year even if we're not so deserving, because we have become a necessary part of the Divine plan. And if we can develop a feeling for what it means to be needed, then we can also strive to realize that indeed *all* Jews are necessary; that each of us needs every one of them, and every Jew is indispensable to the world we live in. And that feeling can be a *zechus,* a source of merit and a source of *simchah* in dealing with others and also with ourselves.

Lech Lecha: Standing Apart

One of the most poignant complaints I have ever heard came from a mother whose son had become a *ba'al teshuvah:* "I accept that he wants to live his own life, and I respect his right to choose. But that he will no longer eat in my home and he will not attend the wedding of his own sister because she is marrying a gentile is just too much for me."

Our knowing the truth of the Torah should not stop us from feeling the pain of this woman, and of many other Jews and gentiles, who find that Torah appears to create barriers between them and their observant friends or relatives, in such matters as *kashrus,* Shabbos, the kind of synagogue one will or will not attend, even entertainment ("You won't come to our December 24th office party?").

In trying to explain, we sometimes say that we would like to join in, but because of religious reasons we cannot; as if the *mitzvah* is a type of allergy or disability which prevents our participating. But as we learn more, we discover that this social separation is not merely a side effect of *mitzvos*, but is a major purpose in itself. *Behold, it is a people which dwells alone, and does not count itself among the nations (Numbers 23:9). And I have separated you from among the nations (Leviticus 20:24).* "Who separates between light and darkness, between Israel and the nations."

Rav Meir Simchah of Dvinsk explained that the division between Jew and gentile is permanent; when Jews attempt to assimilate, it causes anti-Semitism, to remind us of the eternal differences. At the turn of the twentieth century (more than three decades prior to the advent of Hitler), he wrote: Many Jews, in their desire to copy gentiles, have made Berlin their Jerusalem; but it will someday cause a hurricane, to separate us once again.

Like anything else in life, separation must be conducted according to the guidelines of the Torah, not according to what we think it should be. We know the Torah wants us to be loyal citizens, good neighbors, and helpful and cordial to everyone we meet. But at the same time, there are many restrictions especially designed to prevent our becoming too close to non-Jews, from *halachos* which prohibit us from entering churches to the *halachah* that wine touched by gentiles becomes non-kosher.

This standing apart goes all the way back to our father Avraham. When his nephew Lot was taken prisoner by an invading army, it says the news was brought to Avram *Halvri,* Avram the Hebrew. The simple meaning of *Ivri* is a descendant of Noah's grandson Ever. But the Midrash explains that Avraham was given this title because the word *Ever* literally means "side," and *Ivri,* "Hebrew," is: He who stands to the side, apart. Avram *Halvri,* Avram Who Stood Apart, as the Midrash puts it: "The whole world on one side, and Avraham on the other."

We tend to forget that Avraham was the most revolutionary figure in human history. The world believed in a multitude of gods, graven images, and human sacrifice. Infanticide was common, as was the murder of strangers and the elderly. Charity, hospitality, and the decision to serve one invisible Creator Who guides the world with love were radically new ideas introduced by Avraham. Surely, he was not always popular. He must certainly have been accused of extremism and divisiveness, and of destroying communal harmony. But as someone once said: Truth is never more resplendent than when defying moral fashion. The world stood on one side, our *zayde* on the other, and that remains our job even today.

At the same time, we must understand: The Torah says we are to be *a kingdom of priests or princes* (*Exodus* 19:6). And we are to be *a light unto the nations* (*Isaiah* 49:6). Doesn't this standing apart interfere with our national mission? How can the Jew influence his gentile neighbor if the Torah does not allow him to become "one of the guys?"

I once passed a roadside bar-and-grill which had posted a sign: Free Soft Drinks for the Designated Driver, meaning, when a group of beer-buddies arrives for dinner, one person who volunteers to abstain from alcohol is given all the Coca-Cola he desires, so that he can drive his drunken friends home without getting them all killed in an automobile accident.

Imagine the scene at that dinner after the third or fourth round of drinks, when the inebriated company express their sorrow that their friend does not join in. They might even make fun of him or criticize his holier-than-thou attitude of sobriety. But the Designated Driver understands: In order for all of us to travel safely, *I* must abstain; for all of us to stay together, *I* must be different. This does not mean the isolation of a misanthropic hermit but the careful safeguarding of one's own faculties, to ensure that he will be able to continue to serve those who need him most.

Avraham Avinu *called out in the Name of Hashem* (Genesis 12:8; 13:4; 21:33), and thousands heard his call. Gentiles called him *Nesi Elokim,* the Prince of G-d. But he achieved that honor only because they recognized that this was indeed a prince, someone a cut above the rest.

It is surprising how, sometimes, the only way we can come to know another person is by standing apart. Psychologists who become emotionally involved in their clients' problems often lose the objectivity required to be able to give sound advice; and it is a truism that we cannot correctly evaluate ourselves, because we are just too close.

But those who live with Torah and who stand separated from the world in the appropriate measure can truly see the goodness which is *in* the world, like the great Rav Nosson Tzvi Finkel of Slobodka, who looked at every non-Jew as someone created in the image of G-d, which he truly is. The Jew from his vantage point has the perspective to see greatness in the gentile which the gentile himself does not see. We learn this also in the *sidrah.* Avraham is called *Ivri,* he who stands apart, when he hears that his nephew Lot has been kidnaped. Why was this special name mentioned in this particular incident?

Avraham and Lot had previously lived together as one family, until Avraham saw that his nephew condoned dishonesty in his shepherds. Avraham then "stood apart," and they went their separate ways. Lot moved to the wicked city of Sodom, and now he had been kidnaped. It was the most natural thing for Avraham to say: Serves him right! Instead, Avraham risked his own life to save his no-good nephew. The Midrash adds: Avraham risked his life not out of mere family loyalty (there is probably no *mitzvah* to endanger oneself for such a relative), but because Avraham prophetically saw that someday the righteous Ruth would descend from Lot.

We can ask: Even if Lot had been sold into slavery, he could still be an ancestor to Ruth! But perhaps the Midrash means: Avraham, with all his criticism of Lot, was still able to see the spark of goodness in the man, a potential for great things in the future, a potential of which Lot himself may have been unaware. Most of us overlook the faults in those we love, and we see no virtues in those who make us angry. But Avraham stood *apart;* never accepting the bad, and yet never allowing the bad to obscure the good which remained.

So if non-Jewish friends ask why we are not going Trick-or-Treating, give whatever answer you feel is appropriate. But for ourselves, let us remember that we are not deprived or disadvantaged, or forbidden any of the true joys of life. Rather, we are a people apart, committed to a higher ideal. We do not always live up to the standard. But the standard remains as a lighthouse in the storm; pointing the way and preparing a fire which will someday provide light and warmth for the entire world.

Vayeira: The Joys of Social Pressure

Certain words and phrases in the Torah are sometimes open to more than one interpretation, and it is common for classic commentators to disagree on the meaning of a particular passage. Since Hashem could certainly have expressed Himself unambiguously and yet He chose ambiguity, this is to teach us that both Torah interpretations are correct (heard from *Rav Avigdor Miller*). The original story happened only one way, but whatever lessons we can learn from either interpretation are lessons Hashem wants us to learn.

When Avraham and Sarah came to the land of the Philistines they did not reveal that they were married, for fear that someone would kill Avraham to take Sarah. When the Philistine king abducted Sarah, and Hashem made miracles to save her, she was set free. The king asked Avraham: *What did you see* (*Genesis* 20:10) to make you fear us, that you felt you had to hide the truth of your relationship?

Avraham replied: *The one thing missing here is that there is no fear of Elokim, and they would therefore kill me for my wife* (*Genesis* 20:11). Commentaries offer two different interpretations of the word *Elokim*, which means that both interpretations teach us a truth. *Rashi, Malbim* and *Onkelos* explain *yiras Elokim* to mean fear of Hashem. The king may be a man of culture, and his nation may even possess a system of ethics. But without fear of the Divine, humanist ethics are not powerful enough to restrain the passions, and there is danger to innocent people.

However, *Sforno* translates *Elokim* as "the judge," or "governmental authority." This is the literal meaning of the word *Elokim*, applied to Hashem because He is the Supreme Judge. "The one thing missing is that there is no fear of *Elokim*. Philistines do not fear their judges or police; therefore, murder can occur." The Philistines had a very weak central government, as we find later when the Philistine Goliath said, "You Israelites serve King Saul, but I am a Philistine," meaning that he was subservient to no one.

Some studies have shown that to deter crime, the severity of punishment is not nearly as important as is the degree of certainty that the criminal will indeed *be* punished. Those who expect to be caught are unlikely to commit crimes, while those who think they will get away with it are not deterred by even the most severe punishments on the books. Avraham argued that Philistine anarchy, even if it was civilized anarchy, remained a clear and present danger.

The Torah records only a few quotations from our father Avraham, and the few that are mentioned must be of great significance. The importance of this one is: Our ideal is to keep the Torah and to do what is right *because* it is right, because it is Hashem's will. Ideally, we perform *mitzvos* and avoid sin because we choose to, not from any outside pressure. However, here the Torah is telling us, that with all the idealism, we remain human. And for us humans to live up to our own ideals, we must also be subjected to some degree of *external* pressure as well.

Mishnah *Avos* tells us: *Pray for the welfare of the government for if not for fear of it, men would swallow one another alive* (*Avos* 3:2). "Men" means even Jewish men (and likely, women too). We are not savages, but when push comes to shove, all moral principles are strengthened by the knowledge that there is also a policeman waiting down the street.

Two hundred years ago, virtually all Jews were Torah observant. Not everyone was a natural *tzaddik,* but in a society where *mitzvos* were the norm, social pressure to conform kept Jews Jewish. In nineteenth-century Europe, *Yiddishkeit* was more likely to disintegrate in large cities, where there was more anonymity and not the same pressure as on small-town Main Street. (As Rav Yitzchak Hutner *z.l.* put it, "Once a town has two *shuls*, a Jew has the option of attending neither.") The classic ethical guide *Chovos HaLevavos* writes that if not for feelings of embarrassment, children would not usually honor parents, and charity would seldom be given.

It is not that people are hypocrites. People are weak, and we need the encouragement of others to bring out the best in us. The Torah makes a point of telling us this principle in order to urge us to seek out ways to utilize it, to grow as Jews and human beings.

For instance: For someone who is new to the practice of *tefillah* and who finds himself tempted to skip a day, the most effective exercise is not to learn more about the importance of prayer. Instead, he should make it a habit to go daily to *shul*, preferably to a small, friendly *minyan*. Once he is a regular, even if he is tempted to sleep late and thinks Hashem will not notice, he knows that the *gabbai* of the *minyan* and all the other regulars *will* notice, and that will strengthen his resolve to get up and do what he knows he should.

Another example: We all know that *lashon hara* (slanderous gossip, even if the facts are correct) is morally repugnant, and forbidden by the Torah. But being human, we slip, again and again. The best solution to this problem is to form a group of friends to meet regularly to study the writings of the Chofetz Chaim on proper speech, an anti-gossip support group. The reason why it is successful is not so much the study, but it is the embarrassment of being part of the group and feeling ashamed to admit failure in front of your friends. This method even assists those outside the group itself. I was invited to give a talk to one of these Chofetz Chaim assemblies, and the invitation alone encouraged me to watch my tongue for days, out of embarrassment of telling others what to do when I am not careful enough myself.

If you have no external pressure from society, you can sometimes create your own. People occasionally register for adult-education classes and then change their minds, but they attend anyway because they have already paid and don't want to feel their money was wasted. That is a useful approach. Invest time and money in a *shiur,* purchase expensive textbooks and attend the first few sessions, and that will give you an impetus to see it through.

Here is one more example. We know that each of the 613 *mitzvos* is a separate obligation, and therefore negligence in one *mitzvah* is no reason to neglect others. Even someone who works on Shabbos should still not shop on Shabbos. A non-kosher home is no reason to neglect going to the *mikveh,* and a man who does not *daven* should still seize the *mitzvah* of putting on *tefillin* each weekday. I was questioned regarding a gentleman from a non-observant background who had begun keeping Shabbos and covering his head, and who now wished to begin wearing his *yarmulke* in public. However, he was not yet that careful about *kashrus,* and his question was: When he goes into Mineo's Authentic *Treifah* Pizza Shop, should he take off his *yarmulke*? Rav Moshe Feinstein *z.l.* was asked a similar question, and answered that (if for some reason the fellow cannot wear a baseball cap) the *yarmulke* should stay on. But the truth is that if a Jewish man *does* wear his *yarmulke* regularly, the day will surely come when he will no longer feel comfortable patronizing Mineo's.

Fear of Hashem and fear of human punishment or embarrassment are both required; and both interpretations of the passage, *The one thing missing here is that there is no fear of Elokim*, are related.

The Gemara says that to properly perform the *mitzvah* of fearing one's parents, one must fear the One Who gave the commandment to fear them. *Sefer HaChinuch* wrote that the opposite is also true, that reverence for parents will teach us to feel reverence for Hashem. It works both ways. And therefore *Mishlei*, the Book of Proverbs, tells us: *My son, fear the Lord and the king* (*Proverbs* 24:21), because the combination of the Heavenly and earthly monarchs will keep us out of trouble, each one strengthening feelings for the other.

We don't have many earthly kings today. But by creating our own social pressure when appropriate, not to go against our principles but to strengthen those principles we already have, will help us to do what we know we should do. It will also be an exercise to remind us that there *is* Someone above, keeping an eye on us, and we hope to act in a way to make Him, and our father Avraham and mother Sarah, all very, very proud.

Toldos: Yaakov and Eisav

Rivkah Imeinu was expecting twins. The prophet told her, *Within you are two nations* (*Genesis* 25:23), the founders of two great peoples: Yaakov, and Eisav the father of the nation of Edom. From our tradition it appears that some Edomite warriors ended up in Italy, and the Roman patrician class was populated by Eisav's descendants, which means that Eisav and his children were the architects of Western Civilization as we know it.

But the prophecy to Rivkah also said: *The older son will serve the younger* (*ibid*.). Eisav's children fulfill their prophetic destiny by serving Israel. What is the service? Edom hated us, Rome conquered us, and it is said that all the great Jew-haters descend from Eisav. So, apart from a short time when Edom was controlled by ancient Israel, in what way does Eisav serve us?

We often associate "serving" with servants, subservient workers who obey a master. But most professions provide a service, and even kings can choose to use their power to serve their people. The Midrash points out that the prophecy of "two nations" is spelled in the Torah with a letter *yud* instead of a *vav*, and can be pronounced, *"shnei geyim,"* which means: two men of *power*. The prophecy hinted that Rivkah's descendants would include two supremely powerful leaders; and the Midrash says this refers to R' Yehudah HaNasi (Rabbi Judah the Prince) and to the Roman Emperor Antoninus (possibly Marcus Aurelius, the famous "philosopher king").

The Torah alludes to these two, because they symbolize the ideal relationship between Yaakov and Eisav. R' Yehudah met Antoninus (probably on a visit to Rome about the year 165), and the Roman, a seeker of wisdom, recognized the greatness of this Rabbi from the east. When he became Emperor he abolished the anti-Semitic decrees and gave R' Yehudah great honor, including Roman soldiers as personal bodyguards. Because of this gentile, R' Yehudah was able to assemble all the outstanding Torah Sages to compose the Mishnah which is the basis of our lives even today. This was the accomplishment of Yaakov and Eisav, working together.

But surely the prophecy does not refer to only one case. When the Torah says two *peoples*, and the older serving the younger, that defines an ongoing relationship. R' Yehudah and Antoninus were an ideal, and when *Mashiach* comes, the ideal will be fully realized. But until then, if Eisav's purpose is to serve, 3,600 years have passed, and that's an awfully long time to wait to get served.

Perhaps the meaning is: The Gemara says that Hashem will someday proclaim, "Whoever studied Torah, let him come for the reward." Eisav's children will run to the head of the line, saying: "We built roads and bridges and cities, and all that we did was to help Jews study Torah." The cities were for *yeshivos*, and the roads and bridges were to help Torah students get there. Hashem will reply: "Fools! You did it only for yourselves! You built bridges to collect money from tolls. You built cities to create centers of immoral entertainment"; and they will be thrown out.

How could Eisav's descendants have the *chutzpah* to tell the Almighty an outright lie to His face, to say, "We built cities for Torah study?" And why did Hashem reply by calling them fools, and not liars? *The Brisker Rav* explained: They are fools indeed, but their words are not lies. They are fools to think that G-d will reward them, when their intent was only selfish wickedness. But they are not liars, because what they said is correct: All that they build truly *is* for the sake of the Jewish people and for the study of Torah.

There are righteous gentiles who have helped us intentionally, like Emperor Antoninus or Raoul Wallenberg (the Swedish diplomat whose efforts saved thousands of Hungarian Jews during the Holocaust). But even the world in general, intentionally or not, as it makes progress in science and technology, breakthroughs in medicine and physics and all forms of "building," whatever the intent is, it is all being guided by Hashem. New discoveries occur because the Almighty desires them; if He did not, one nuclear war would suffice to return us to the Dark Ages. But Hashem wants these discoveries, because knowledge can benefit the world. And the most important benefit is to help fulfill the *purpose* of the world: Torah learning, *mitzvos*, and nobility of character.

In the mid-1960's, Mesivtha Tifereth Jerusalem opened a branch in Staten Island soon after completion of the Verrazano-Narrows Bridge, which connects the island with Brooklyn. At that time a rabbi said: "People think that a side benefit of the new bridge is that it allowed us to build a *yeshivah*. They have it backwards. The truth is because G-d wanted a *yeshivah* in Staten Island, He gave the non-Jews the technology to build the bridge in the first place."

This writer was reminded of that statement when he attended a Mesivtha Tifereth Jerusalem dinner in the late 1980's, after the passing of the *Rosh Yeshivah* Rav Moshe Feinstein *z.l.* At the dinner, the committee played a videotape recording of the *Rosh Yeshivah* speaking and giving his *brachah*. To those who knew the *Rosh Yeshivah*, the video was no substitute. But imagine, what would people pay to see a videotape of the Baal Shem Tov or the Chofetz Chaim! And we are the ones who are *zocheh* to live in the age of such inventions that the voices and pictures of our teachers remain, to inspire us and generations yet to come.

The Japanese video company which made the tape was not thinking about the *Rosh Yeshivah,* but Hashem was, and is, and that is why we have such a marvelous tool today. Eisav cares only for himself. But Hashem plans history, so that Eisav's work should also work for us. How much time and money did corporations invest to develop the equipment which now produces audio and videotapes of Torah *shiurim*? Or the cable television on which *chassidim* see their *rebbe*? Or the word-processors on which *sefarim* are composed? Or the programming which makes it possible for computers to check *Sifrei Torah* for mistakes?

Every bridge and road, every advance in medicine, every new creation of Eisav has eternal value, in whatever way it helps us to learn and keep the Torah. The older brother truly does serve the younger, and someday, when Eisav asks for a reward for all the good he did, he won't be a liar. But he's a fool, for not realizing it right now, and for not including that eternal purpose in his intent.

Eisav is a fool, but we don't have to be. We can use our eyes to look at the world, especially all the discoveries of recent years, to see in them how each one advances the cause of Torah. We can use our brains to realize that if we don't use those discoveries for Torah purposes, we are wasting all of Eisav's work and the entire world.

You own a VCR, and you don't own Torah videotapes? You drive the interstate highway system, or the Verrazano Bridge, and you never visit the major *yeshivos*? At least let us have compassion for all the work the non-Jews put in, and let the efforts count for something.

Recognizing life's profundity, and that each person has a purpose in Hashem's world, will make all of us happier and holier, more at peace with the world and with ourselves. It is tragic that Eisav does not appreciate his opportunities to serve. At least let us appreciate our own opportunities; so that when the day comes that Hashem proclaims "Whoever studied Torah, let him come for the reward," we should then be able to join the line and to remain there forever, with pride.

Vayishlach: Divine Apologies

On Rosh Chodesh, the first day of the month, the Torah commands us to bring an offering of *lechatas laShem* (*Numbers* 28:15), a term which can be translated in more than one way. The simple meaning is "for a sin-offering brought to Hashem," an offering we bring on Rosh Chodesh to atone for our sins.

But the Midrash suggests a different translation, that *lechatas laShem* means a sin-offering brought to atone *for* Hashem for wrongs committed by Him, *chas veshalom*. What did Hashem do wrong that He requires atonement? The Midrash's explanation tells a story, which (*Rishonim* tell us) is not necessarily meant to be taken literally, but which has a profound allegorical meaning.

When the sun and moon were first created, the Torah says: *Hashem created the two great lights, the great light to rule the day, and the small light to rule the night* (Genesis 1:16). This seems to contradict itself. It first says there were *two great lights,* and then it refers to the moon as *the small light.* Was the moon great, or small? The Midrash answers:

Originally, the moon was also great; the sun and moon were the same size. But the moon complained: I and the sun are like two monarchs ruling the world as partners; that's no way to run things, two kings sharing a single crown. Hashem responded to the complaint by reducing the moon's size.

The moon protested, "Master of the World, because I said something logical, must I lose as a result?" The Creator replied that He would give the moon a consolation prize, all the stars, but the moon was not satisfied. The Creator offered the honor that Israel will determine its holidays by a lunar calendar, but whatever He said was still not enough. Finally, the Creator said: "What can I do? On Rosh Chodesh, the first day of the month when the new moon appears, bring an offering to atone for Me, that I hurt the moon's feelings by diminishing its size."

We do not know the full depth of meaning in that Midrash, but there are at least two lessons that are immediately obvious. Lesson #1: Don't complain. The moon was unwilling to share; it protested, and it ended up with less than it had at the start. Lesson #2: Hashem diminished the moon's size, and He surely had good reason for doing so. However, since this act caused the moon's feelings to be hurt, Hashem acknowledged even *He* requires an atonement.

Every Rosh Chodesh there was an offering in the *Beis HaMikdash* as a reminder, a lesson in *derech eretz.* Sometimes we do things that hurt others, and we may even be justified in what we do. It may even be for the other person's benefit, like a parent or a teacher disciplining a child. Nevertheless, Rosh Chodesh teaches us: Inside, we have to feel that other person's

Vayishlach: Divine Apologies

pain; we must feel that we need atonement if another is hurt because of us, no matter how correct we might be.

The *parashah* tells us the tragic story of Yaakov Avinu's daughter Dinah, who was attacked and abducted by Shechem. The Midrash discusses what sin Dinah might have committed to deserve her terrible fate, and the Midrash also asks what sin Yaakov Avinu committed that warranted this tragedy.

The answer for Yaakov Avinu was: When he met his brother Eisav after a twenty-year separation, Yaakov introduced him to all his sons, but Yaakov kept his daughter Dinah hidden from view. He was afraid that Eisav might ask for her hand in marriage. Hashem said: What kind of brother are you? If Dina married Eisav, she might have made a *mentch* out of him. You were unwilling to give her away in marriage; you will lose her, in a more terrible way.

What does the Midrash mean? Am I supposed to let Eisav marry my daughter? Should I encourage my children to marry criminals in the hope of reforming them? Certainly not. But the great Rav Simcha Zissel Ziv explained that Hashem agreed, surely you have no choice but to hide your daughter from Eisav. But at the same time, do you feel badly about it? Do you say, "*Oy*, if only I could save my brother and give him Dinah as a wife. Of course it is out of the question, but if only . . .?" Yaakov protected his daughter, as he was obligated to do. But because he did not feel the other side of the coin, because he did not also feel strongly enough for Eisav, he is blamed.

This is a lofty ideal. But it is something for all of us to remember, at least once a month, every Rosh Chodesh. In the past month, did we hurt anyone's feelings? Even for the best of reasons, we should still feel at least a little bit guilty about it. Perhaps we had no choice; but we should feel a desire to atone and learn from Hashem's example. This is true when we cause pain to friends and acquaintances, to children and to spouses; and, perhaps we can take the liberty of suggesting, this is true even when we cause pain to ourselves.

The day before Rosh Chodesh is traditionally a day of repentance, known as *Yom Kippur Kattan*, a miniature Yom

Kippur. On that day some people fast, and confess their sins in prayer. But the very next day, on Rosh Chodesh itself, we sing the song of *Hallel*, and in the *Shemoneh Esrei* we proclaim that it is a time of atonement for all our sins.

Yesterday I was confessing, yesterday I was admitting my shortcomings. Today I must remind myself that I am more than the sum total of my feelings, and therefore every Rosh Chodesh is a day to make a new start, a new beginning in life; new in the way I treat others, and in the way I treat myself.

Tonight, when you see the moon outside, let it be a reminder: Be happy with what you have. Don't complain. Be willing to share the glory.

And on Rosh Chodesh, when you are grumpily thinking how long *davening* takes, with all its extra *tefillos*, remember: The extra *davening* commemorates the extra sacrificial offering, because Rosh Chodesh is a time when even Hashem desires atonement; a time to consider if perhaps we have hurt anyone's feelings, even with good cause; because Rosh Chodesh, with all its extra *mitzvos*, is a good time to remember to be extra good.

Vayishlach: Divine Apologies

Vayechi:
Cultural Bondage

Among the lessons taught by the story of Yosef and his brothers is that parents should take care not to display favoritism for one child over another. As the Gemara says, because Yaakov gave Yosef a bit of colored cloth, our ancestors ended up in Egypt. Why then, in *Parshas Vayechi*, did our father Yaakov give special blessings to Yosef's sons Ephraim and Menashe, blessings granted to no other grandchild? Wasn't he concerned about the reaction of the rest of the family?

Rav Yaakov Kamenetzky *z.l.* answered: The brothers understood that Yosef's children needed those special blessings, because only Yosef's children were born in Egypt. The other grandchildren had been born in *Eretz Yisrael*, and raised in a totally Jewish environment. Ephraim and Menashe, although they were the sons of a perfect *tzaddik*, were surrounded by the corrupting influence of Egyptian society. In such cases some detrimental effect is virtually inevitable, and one needs an extra blessing not to abandon the Torah.

Rav Yaakov offered a boldly original illustration of the Egyptian influence surrounding Yosef. He suggested that Egyptian nobility took names related to the name of Pharaoh. The *Chumash* mentions the names Poti*Phar* and Poti*Phera*. The chief midwife was Shi*Phrah*, *shin-phei-resh-hei,* three out of the four letters in the Hebrew name "Pharaoh." Her assistant was Puah, *pei-vau-ayin-hei,* again three letters out of the four. Pharaoh himself named Yosef Pa'ane'ach, *pey* and *ayin* as in Pharaoh. And, Rav Yaakov noted, Yosef named his second son E*phra*im, once again with a *phei* and a *resh*. The name Ephraim certainly has meaning in Hebrew, but Rav Yaakov suggested that the name was also Egyptian, and a bit of an accommodation to the host culture.

Yosef was a towering giant of virtue and holiness, far beyond our abilities to comprehend. Even so, one cannot live in a pagan environment without something rubbing off. This is a well-known Torah principle, though Rav Yaakov's specific theory of nomenclature is quite novel. Working from his theory, that Egyptian influence was seen in names, we can also learn where the danger of pagan influence first tends to manifest itself.

In a non-Jewish society, especially in a free society, we tend to adopt the status symbols of our neighbors. In deeds, Yosef did not deviate from Torah an inch. But in public honors, in naming his child, he was (for whatever reason, possibly including Torah reasons) drawn after the fashion of calling his son "Child of Pharaoh"; and, according to Rav Yaakov, this was already a beginning of assimilation.

Surely the Torah records this as a warning to ourselves. We must be cordial neighbors, loyal citizens, and appreciative of all the blessings of the nation in which we live. But at the same time, we must remain vigilantly on guard against any loss of Jewish pride which makes us view ourselves only through the eyes of gentiles, and which leads us to seek status and self-respect through non-Jewish definitions of success.

Articles in American-Jewish newspapers from the early 1900's display a passion for attaining the goal of not being considered a "greenhorn," an unAmericanized newcomer. The editor of the Yiddish Daily Forward published a list of English words to use when speaking Yiddish (!), to show that one was "with it," properly American. It is told that a great rabbi moved from Russia to New York City, and in his maiden sermon he made sure to use the appropriate English words. However, in the middle of the *drashah* he committed the terrible *faux pas* of pulling out his European-style colored handkerchief, causing great embarrassment; because Jews were viewing themselves through the eyes of others, and exchanging pride in Torah for a white handkerchief and a derby hat.

Ethnic pluralism is more acceptable today, but the problem still exists. Consider the "Fruppy," the Frum Young Urban Professional: financially successful, *Shomer Shabbos*, active *shul* member, who is at the same time a loyal follower of Esquire or Cosmopolitan magazine, and who sees no contradiction between his or her spiritual ideals and materialistic life-style. Can we truly "have it all?" And just what is that "it" that we Jews should want to have?

When the Egyptian bondage began, the Midrash says Israel took an oath that even in slavery they would continue to speak their own language, wear only their own distinctive clothing, and use only Hebrew names. Today, *halachah* permits us to speak English, and (according to many authorities) it is not required to wear distinctly different Jewish dress or use only Hebrew names. Rav Moshe Feinstein *z.l.* suggested that back then, when Israel did not yet have the Torah to separate us from gentile society, and when they realized their original mistake of trying to become Egyptianized, they said: Our only hope for survival is to keep alive *all* our cultural differences, even little things which make us distinct as a people.

Today, although it is praiseworthy to use our own language and garb and names, it is no longer vital to the same degree, because Torah itself makes us unique. But we must be perceptive enough to recognize the values of American Egypt which confront us, and not to fall into the trap of appropriating Pharaonic status symbols as our own. We are part of society, and we enjoy its material benefits. But our heart, our pride, must be in other things, higher things, in enjoying and perpetuating the blessings of our father Yaakov and his sons.

Shemos: Passing On

Hakaras hatov (or hakaras tovah), the obligation to express gratitude to one's benefactors, is a famous fundamental Torah principle. The Egyptians enslaved us, but we are commanded by the Torah not to despise them, because they gave us hospitality in their land. The Midianites attacked us, but Moshe Rabbeinu did not lead the battle against them in person, because he had found refuge in Midian when he fled from Pharaoh. All this is well known. But *Parashas Shemos* tells of a qualitatively different kind of gratitude, a level of *hakaras hatov* beyond everything to which we are accustomed.

Moshe Rabbeinu was taken out of the Nile River as a baby. He grew up, went out to his people, and rescued a Hebrew slave by killing his Egyptian attacker. The next day, he saved another Jew who was being attacked by his fellow man. Moshe then had to flee, and when he arrived in Midian he came to the aid of utter strangers, Yisro's daughters, saving them from marauding shepherds. It is all very noble. But one must wonder, was Moshe Rabbeinu a one-man police department? Was he a Biblical Sir Galahad who went looking for men and damsels in distress, that he was continually rescuing them?

Perhaps any *tzaddik* would have done the same; but it is odd that we do not find similar rescue operations in the lives of the Patriarchs, except once or twice when their own families were threatened. Moshe Rabbeinu is known as the teacher, not the warrior. Why was it his speciality, or perhaps his destiny, to be the savior, time and again?

When Pharaoh's daughter saved the Hebrew baby's life, she named him Moshe,"*ki min hamayim meshisihu,* for I have drawn him up from the water." The word Moshe literally means "one who *draws* up," and Rabbi Samson Raphael Hirsch asked: Since Moshe was the one who was rescued, Pharaoh's daughter should have named him *Mashuy,* the one who was *drawn*. Why Moshe, the one who draws?

The answer is: Moshe, your life was saved. Repay the favor, by dedicating your life to saving others. You were drawn up from death? Then you yourself must become the *Moshe,* someone who goes out of his way to help another, and to pull others out from the dangers that engulf them.

We see here a general principle. *Hakaras tovah,* the obligation of gratitude, is not only to return a favor to the benefactor. It also includes taking the kindness, whatever goodness comes your way, and passing it on, to others who need it as well. The Gemara tells of an elderly man who planted a fruit tree, and he was asked: Do you expect to live long enough to eat its fruit? He replied: Those who came before me planted trees that I enjoy today; so I too plant, for others to enjoy tomorrow.

Shemos: Passing On

The Gemara also says that one should not take money for teaching Torah. I might have thought the reason is that we should not use a sacred gift from Hashem for personal gain, but the Gemara gives a different reason. Just as Moshe Rabbeinu taught us Torah without compensation, so too we should do the same. Even without the reason of sanctity, even without the divinity in Torah, the very fact that Moshe Rabbeinu taught us all as a gift is reason enough for us to do likewise.

This is an idea which can make a powerful impact on our everyday lives, because all of us receive many thousands of kindnesses we cannot repay: the love of parents and grandparents no longer with us, help from teachers in the past, friends, neighbors, even perfect strangers who give us directions, or the correct time, or a passing smile. Whatever we receive should be viewed as an investment, and it should produce dividends which we dole out to others in the long run. You were pulled out of a mess, you were *Mashuy?* Then become a *Moshe*, someone who pulls out others as well.

When I hear of airplane crashes and auto accidents, all the people who did not have a chance to live out their lives, I am reminded of a young student at the great Lithuanian *yeshivah* of Slabodka, who was murdered by the Nazis. In 1932, when one of my teachers came to Slabodka as a young man, this student went out of his way to extend hospitality to him.

My teacher repaid the kindness later on, by applying the lessons in hospitality he had learned to those who visited him, so that I myself benefited from this student who died long before I was born. Today, I in turn try to repay both of them, by applying some of those same lessons to those who visit me.

The Midrash says that Pharaoh's daughter Basya, through her act of kindness, earned the merit to be converted to Judaism, which is why even today Jewish children are named after her. All of us, by becoming *Moshim,* those who help others, can thereby remind ourselves of all the blessings we have received in the past; to keep the blessings from growing stale, to enjoy them and relive them every day, together with all those other good people with whom we share this world.

Vaeira:
Public Protests

At the first of the Ten Plagues, Moshe Rabbeinu is commanded: Speak to Aaron, tell him to stretch forth his hand over the waters of Egypt, and the waters will turn to blood. *Rashi* quotes the Midrash that Moshe was not told to stretch out his own hand, because the Nile had sheltered him as an infant, and it was not fitting that Moshe do it harm. Even for the sake of a *mitzvah*, it is appropriate that Aaron be the one to harm the Nile. This is a famous lesson in the importance of gratitude, to feel grateful even eighty years after the event, and even if the benefactor (in this case, the Nile) could not know the difference one way or the other.

At the second plague, once again Moshe is commanded: Speak to Aaron, to make the river swarm with frogs. Again *Rashi* explains, it was not proper for Moshe to personally cause the Nile to become infested. Again at the third plague, Moshe is commanded: Speak to Aaron, to strike the earth and turn it to lice. *Rashi* explains that since the earth had protected Moshe when he killed the Egyptian taskmaster and buried him in the sand, Aaron again should substitute.

To teach this lesson, once would suffice. If *Chumash* repeats it three times, clearly something more is being hinted at. Perhaps that something is: Every sin has some root cause, a defect of character or faith which is the source of the destructive behavior. What caused Pharaoh to enslave us? The Torah says: "A new king arose over Egypt who did not know Joseph." *Rashi* quotes different opinions whether it was truly a new king or a change of heart in the old one. Either way, how could he not have known about Joseph, the national hero who saved the country and vastly increased Pharaoh's treasury and power? *Rashi* adds: "who did not know — he made himself *as if* he did not know." The fundamental crime was a lack of gratitude, and that led in a natural progression to all the other crimes which followed.

Therefore, when Hashem sent the plagues, He said: Moshe, don't you strike the water or the dust. Don't be like Pharaoh. Demonstrate that *you* have not forgotten, show gratitude even to inanimate objects, to display your inner feelings of appreciation again and again.

Perhaps this is intended as a general Torah principle: When facing spiritual evil, it becomes our obligation to work to strengthen that same specific type of spirituality, for good. The Gemara tells of a man who possessed an unusually long beard, and who gave a reason for it: תְּהֵא כְּנֶגֶד הַמַּשְׁחִיתִים, which the Chofetz Chaim translated as "Let my beard be against [i.e. atone for] those who shave with razors!" When others were transgressing the Torah by shaving with razors, *this* man grew a beard that was extra long, to counter them.

These are true Jewish forms of protest: a long beard in

opposition to those who shave with razors; gratitude to a river, to display protest against a Pharaoh who has no gratitude to those who saved him and his people. Pharaoh himself may or may not grasp the symbolism. But the main purpose of the protest is for ourselves, that we endeavor to keep the positive spiritual value from getting lost.

Rav Yisrael Salanter taught that holiness has a ripple effect, and avoiding *lashon hara* in Kovna helps Jews in Paris hold on to the Shabbos. All the more so in the same *mitzvah*, that refraining from *lashon hara* will have a beneficial impact on our neighbors. This is a response of spiritual protest, and one which is always appropriate.

And, let us suggest, the very best time to use this response is when someone makes us angry.

If someone acts rudely towards you, protest! Not by being rude in return, but by being extra polite to the very next person you meet. If you gave a gift and never received a thank-you note, learn from Moshe Rabbeinu to discover new ways to express appreciation yourself, perhaps by writing your own letter of thanks to some benefactor who deserves one.

Most of what we call "righteous indignation" contains two elements: We are upset that people act unjustly, and we are much *more* upset that the object of their injustice was ourselves. If we give in to the temptation to get back at them by acting just like them, we ultimately ruin the moral sensitivity which gave us the righteous indignation in the first place. Like the man who tried to get through winter by cutting out pieces of wood from his roof to put in his fireplace, each new piece just made the house that much colder.

Instead, if our response to anger is to act impeccably to the next person we meet, we thereby seize the moral high ground, and we gain a victory by demonstrating that goodness lives on in the world. There are thousands of opportunities to do this. If someone disturbs you in *shul*, take it as impetus to concentrate ten minutes on your own *davening* without interruption. If the young man behind the supermarket counter is wearing earrings, protest — not by picketing supermarkets, but by treating family and friends with extra love, to demonstrate that healthy unperverted love is a beautiful thing.

If Shabbos desecration in Israel disturbs you, protest, by strengthening the sanctity of your own Shabbos. If violence committed by protesters disturbs you, then protest that too, by expressing differences of opinion you may have with others always in the most polite manner. If you disapprove of the way your *shul* is run, protest, by getting involved yourself. And even if you don't like your rabbi's sermon, protest, by learning an extra fifteen or twenty minutes of Torah on your own to compensate for it.

Moshe Rabbeinu demonstrating gratitude to the Nile may not have had any effect on Pharaoh, but it surely had an impact on *Klal Yisrael*. It set the stage for Mt. Sinai, where Hashem chose to introduce Himself with the words: "I am Hashem your God Who took you out from Egypt," i.e. I am Hashem for you to accept as your God, because of gratitude, your appreciation for My setting you free.

This character trait which Moshe strengthened became the character of the nation as a whole. The name *Yehudi* is from Yehudah, and it means "one who gives thanks." Appreciate the blessings, experience the joys, and live with a conscious recognition that all our joys come directly from the infinite love of Hashem.

Bo: Other People's Foolishness

At the last of the ten plagues, Moshe Rabbeinu foretold that Hashem would smite the Egyptian firstborn *about midnight* (*Exodus* 11:4). Why did he say about midnight; was He unsure of the Almighty's arrival time?

The Gemara explains that Hashem would certainly arrive at the stroke of twelve, but Moshe knew: If the Egyptian timepieces were a bit fast, they might think that midnight has already arrived and there is no plague. Even when the plague did hit five minutes later, apparently it would lose some of its psychological impact; so Moshe told them *about midnight,* give or take a few minutes.

If the prophet is relating truth from Hashem, can he not "tell it like it is?" Must Moshe Rabbeinu make allowances for the listener's foolish errors? We see here that, indeed, he must.

It would appear that the reason for this extreme caution, to take into account even the listener's error, is because Moshe is relating the Word of Hashem; any misunderstanding of the Word detracts from the honor due the Creator. However, our Sages tell us that this vigilance is for everyone, even in mundane conversation. The Gemara says we should learn from Moshe to be in the habit of saying "I don't know, I am not certain," in order not to appear like a liar later on. This means: If asked when the *shiur* or the PTA meeting will begin, we should answer "around 7:30 (or whatever time it is), approximately"; because if we say "7:30" and it begins at 7:45, this affects our whole credibility. It also appears to be saying that even if the meeting *does* begin on time, we should be concerned that the other fellow's watch may be inaccurate, and he will blame us for a discrepancy which exists only in his imagination! This seems rather extreme. If I speak honestly and accurately, why be concerned about a listener's misunderstanding, and his accusation that I said midnight while his watch reads 11:55?

But we find this same principle elsewhere in *halachah*, in the rules of *maris ayin*, avoiding suspicious appearances. For example, clothing which became wet on Shabbos may not be spread out to dry, lest someone suspect us of having washed it on Shabbos. My fellow Jew has his own Torah obligation to judge favorably and not think the worst of me. If I did nothing wrong, why must I refrain from something permitted because of impressions made on a misanthropic curmudgeon?

Perhaps the answer is that honesty, not to deceive or do harm, is basic morality; but our purpose here on earth includes more than merely not causing harm. It is our job to also do positive good, to add to the sum total of kindness and love and joy in the world as best we can, every day. We may not always be able to accomplish great things, but everyone can accomplish a little.

Part of that kindness and love is to try our best to make other people feel at ease, happy with us and with themselves. Our Sages said that in Heaven we are asked: "Did you treat your fellow man like a king?" And therefore, included in our mission of kindliness is the obligation to make an effort to avoid any situation which creates even minor friction, anything that might tear at the delicate social fabric which unites us; to do what we can that others should not be displeased or complaining or accusing, even if the source of the accusation is their own unreasonableness.

Because of this, in most human-relations problems such as quarrels in families and between neighbors, we should generally not focus on the question of who is to *blame*. People seldom blame themselves, and trying to assign guilt only makes matters worse. In addition, seen from a broader perspective, the question of blame is irrelevant. My work as a Jew is to be *rodef shalom,* to pursue peace, and make others comfortable. If my neighbor is at fault, but I can create peace with my own apology, it is well worth doing. If we know sensitive people who become angry or upset over certain subjects, it is simple courtesy for us to avoid such subjects in conversation.

Many people have been conditioned to believe what appears to be the opposite, that they must always be assertive, or even aggressive: "Don't let yourself be stepped on. Don't be a miserable Caspar Milquetoast. If you don't care about yourself, no one else will!" There is nothing wrong with those ideas, but we should realize that they need not contradict the principles of kindness mentioned above.

A woman whose husband has a terrible temper, and who screams at the slightest provocation, once asked my advice. I suggested that a first step is for her to recognize that her husband is suffering, afflicted by stress, and possibly from feelings of insecurity. She should not take his shouting seriously, and she should certainly not answer back in the same tone of voice.

She objected, "Must I allow myself to be a doormat, to let him walk all over me?" I replied: "Of course not. But you should recognize that the other person is suffering from an emotional weakness, or, if you prefer, an illness, and that you do *not* have to react to it, not feel guilty and not counterattack. This recognition means that *you* are in control of your life and that he is *not*. This allows you to reach out in sympathy; and if necessary, to let him throw a temper tantrum until even *he* realizes it won't do him any good, and just makes him look silly."

We should not allow others to ruin our lives, or to take away our self-esteem or personal happiness. But if we feel content with ourselves, that we are the agents of Hashem to make the world a better place, then we will want to accommodate others in a spirit of *noblesse oblige,* generosity concomitant with the high rank of our position.

Moshe Rabbeinu had to rephrase his words to say *about midnight* to allow for Pharaoh's error. Did Moshe complain in frustration: "*Oy*, do I have to worry how Pharaoh will react to every word I say?" Moshe was surely not disturbed by such things, because Hashem had already told him: *I, Hashem, have made you like a Divine Authority to guide Pharaoh* (*Exodus* 7:1). Pharaoh didn't know that, but Moshe did; and with that kind of authority it is easy to make allowances for the poor souls of those Pharaohs who need me.

Try to imagine yourself as an old-time *chassidishe Rebbe*. Not all your followers are learned enough to appreciate your *divrei Torah*, and some of them are simple, unsophisticated people. But when you enter the *shtiebel*, you feel good. Not because everyone stands up for you (remember, you're a *tzaddik*, not a status-seeker) do you feel good, but because you know that you make at least a small difference in the life of every single person there — a greeting, a smile, a compliment, encouragement, occasional advice. Like many *tzaddikim*, your signature reads, "The servant of the servants of Hashem," which you truly are; and which gives you enormous honor and enormous pleasure, knowing that you have been chosen to serve.

Back to reality today: You may not be a *Rebbe*; but everyone you meet is, in some way, your *chassid*. They all need you, you have something to give to each one, even if it's only a "Good Shabbos" and a smile. If you become aware of your exalted position as agent of Hashem in this difficult world, you will find it much, much easier to allow for each person's individual quirks and moral handicaps. You will not excuse all improper behavior. But you will accept the person, as one of your people, given to you to help, to make them feel a bit more at ease; to help add to the mountain of *mitzvos* and love and goodness created by all *tzaddikim;* a mountain going up to Hashem, and leading to redemption for us all.

Yisro: Parents and Adult Children

Parashas *Yisro* contains the *Aseres HaDibros,* the Ten Commandments, including what is perhaps the most difficult of all *mitzvos* to properly perform: *Honor your father and mother (Exodus 19:12).* The Gemara says that to give parents the full honor they deserve is so difficult that only orphans fulfill their obligations. The rest of us almost invariably fall short.

Part of the difficulty in this *mitzvah* is that we owe our parents for the gift of life itself, a gift which is so precious that it cannot be fully repaid. Often, an additional difficulty is that the parent-child relationship begins when the child is small and helpless, and the parent is powerful. This creates a certain relationship, a mindset in both parent and child. When the child grows up to be an independent adult, sometimes an adult who becomes the caregiver for the parent, the change in the relationship can be very hard for them to digest.

Yet another problem is that almost every childhood includes a certain amount of pain; and even the best parents can unintentionally create certain anxieties in their children, a fear or a bitterness which comes from the child's lack of understanding, and which can remain with the child, forever.

The parent should not feel guilty (no one is perfect) and the grown-up child should not be resentful (the childhood given him or her was chosen by Hashem as the very best for him or her). But often, an adult must come to terms with pain he or she may not want to admit; a difficult relationship with parents stretching back to infancy, a problem that may have been only a product of the child's imagination, but which continues to produce pain throughout life.

If you are reading this and you have no idea what it's all about, if you are wondering, "How can anyone feel resentment against a parent? I adore my parents!" — if you feel that way, then good for you, and give thanks to Hashem. But sadly, many adults do bear a resentment from their childhood; whether it is a feeling that they could never measure up to the parent's expectations, or a bitterness of believing that a sibling was more favored, or actual abuse of some kind. The adult may not even be fully conscious of the wound inside. But the pain can add many layers of complexity to the parent-child relationship, and relationship problems between parents and grown children are very common.

What can be done about it? How can we show our parents proper honor if we don't feel loving enough inside? The following is one possible approach:

The Ten Commandments were inscribed on two separate Tablets. Our Sages explain that the first Tablet contains *mitzvos* between us and Hashem, like the *mitzvah* of Shabbos and the prohibition against idolatry; the second Tablet has *mitzvos* between one individual and another, such as "Thou shalt not steal or kill." On which Tablet is the *mitzvah* of honoring father and mother? On the first. It is not placed together with the *mitzvos* between me and my fellow Jew, but is inscribed with the *mitzvos* between me and Hashem.

We can suggest that this is because *love* of parents is a very beautiful thing; but it is not in the Torah as a *commandment*, loving them was not given as an obligation. Love thy neighbor, try to love everyone, certainly. But a special *mitzvah* to love mother and father, a command to do so if you do not feel it? There is no such *mitzvah*. In the same vein, there is no *mitzvah* to love your own children. This is due to the fact that the world of emotions is so private, and so difficult, that the Torah does not presume to command us to feel what we do not (even "Love thy neighbor" and the *mitzvah* to love Hashem are explained by some to mean *actions* of love or to work to try to develop certain attitudes). If you love your mother, that is marvelous. But if you do not, if something went haywire in the relationship, tragic as it is, don't add to your pain by feeling guilty on top of it.

Once we recognize that the Torah is not legislating emotions, we can understand the Gemara's explanation of the *mitzvah* to honor parents. The Gemara interprets "honoring" not as a feeling, but as specific actions and speech and tone of voice. For instance, the *halachah* says that when your parents enter the room, you should stand up. Serve them food and drink, and offer whatever physical assistance will add to their comfort, anything from doing shopping to tying their shoes.

If your mother or father has a specific place at the table or a special chair, do not sit there without their permission. We may not speak harshly to parents, and we may not contradict them to say "you're wrong" even if they are. If we must correct them, it should only by done in a tentative, questioning manner. We have similar obligations towards parents-in-law, and also to a stepparent married to our father or mother.

These are all laws of action, not emotion, because the Torah is not commanding us to feel something we don't. Of course, the goal of the *mitzvah* is not merely to perform mechanical acts of reverence while feeling resentful inside. Surely, there is some thought which should accompany the *mitzvah*.

There is. One underlying idea in honoring parents is: If someone does me kindness, I am obliged to show gratitude. If someone gives me a gift of a set of fine china, I owe them at least a dinner invitation or two. And if my father and my mother give me the gift of life, then I must use my life to express thanks to them, forever.

Everyone agrees that gratitude is part of good character. But the Torah goes further by telling us that we must be grateful, even if our benefactor's motivation was not so sincere. We also owe a debt of thanks even if later on our benefactor turned against us. This is the Will of Hashem, that we should not forget any kindness received. The Torah commands us not to despise an Egyptian, because Egypt gave us hospitality when there was famine in the time of Yosef. The Egyptians did not invite us out of kindness, and afterwards they enslaved us. But with all their wickedness, we are commanded not to forget the goodness received. That is the quality of a noble soul, not to allow the bad to erase all memory of good.

Therefore, we owe those special human beings who brought us into the world — whatever their motivation may have been, and however they treated us afterwards — forever. Whether they are now loving, angry, domineering or helpless, it is our task to treat them with honor. Similar honor is due a stepparent, because honoring them is honor to their spouse. We also show respect to parents-in-law, to express gratitude that they gave birth to our own spouse.

It is proper for each of us to take a few minutes to draw up a list of all the kindnesses received from our parents. They gave you life. Likely, they gave you food, clothing, shelter and medical care. They gave you their time, their effort, and they literally lost sleep over you. They may have made financial sacrifices to send you to school or *yeshivah*, to educate you for the future. Make a list, just to see what it's worth in dollars and cents; not to mention the debt we owe for love.

And when you total up all the benefits received, then you should conclude: I honor my parents, ideally with a desire to do so; but even if the desire is somewhat lacking, I honor them because expressing gratitude in this way is truly the Will of Hashem.

Parents should not fall into the trap of *expecting* gratitude. Such expectations can set you up for a life of heartache. The parent should provide for the child out of love, and from a desire to raise another Jew to serve Hashem; do this *mitzvah* of parenting without asking for reward in this world; and if reward comes, if the child reciprocates the caring and the love, take it as a bonus.

The Gemara says, when Rav Yosef heard his mother approach he would say: The *Shechinah*, the presence of G-d, is coming! With his mother, he felt the presence of Hashem. That is a lofty ideal. But for all of us, even for children who have little feeling, if we keep in mind that honoring parents is on the first Tablet, that it is part of our *mitzvah* to honor Hashem, we can then begin to treat them with the respect they deserve; knowing that this respect is a recognition of the presence of Hashem in our own lives, and in the lives of our own children and grandchildren, who will learn from us to act accordingly.

Terumah: Dishonest and Pious?

I met a young man who was a new employee at a Hebrew book-and-gift shop, a store owned and run by strictly Orthodox people, and he explained that he was in the process of "learning the business." "For instance," he said, "you have to be able to size up the customer; if he wants to buy a *menorah* and he looks wealthy, then — you jack up the price." I looked at the young man in astonishment; he looked astonished at my astonishment; and that was the end of the conversation, until now.

The Torah forbids us to make graven images, statues of humans or angels, even if those images are intended solely as symbols of devotion to Hashem. But in *Parashas Terumah* there is one great exception to this prohibition, and we are commanded, *You shall make two keruvim* of gold (*Exodus* 25:18). In the *Mishkan*, the Sanctuary of the Tabernacle, it was a *mitzvah* to fashion images of two golden angels called *keruvim*, cherubim.

The angels were to rise from either end of the cover on the Ark, the *Aron Kodesh*, which contained the Tablets of the Torah. Their wings should cover the Ark and the two angels should face each other. Hashem said that He would speak with Moshe there; the Divine Voice would emanate from between the two images.

What is the meaning of this *mitzvah*? The Gemara says that the angels had human-like faces, and commentaries explain that they represent the People of Israel. Every Jew is bound to the *Aron Kodesh*, and our great purpose is to cover it, to protect the integrity of the Torah at all times. But why are the angels two in number? Why not one, to symbolize one united people, or perhaps twelve, like the twelve tribes? Why two?

The Malbim answers that the two *keruvim* correspond to the two Tablets brought down from Mount Sinai, which in turn represent two categories of *mitzvos*: *mitzvos* between us and Hashem, and *mitzvos* between one person and another. The first five of the Ten Commandments, inscribed on the first of the two Tablets, are *mitzvos* between us and Hashem: the *mitzvah* of belief; the prohibition against idolatry and blasphemy; the Shabbos, and honoring father and mother, as they are Hashem's representatives. The second Tablet contains social *mitzvos*: not to steal or kill or commit adultery or bear false witness or covet a neighbor's possessions.

Honesty and fidelity are *mitzvah* responsibilities very different from keeping Shabbos or avoiding idols, and the two angels rise from either end of the Ark cover. But both angels are carved out of the same piece of gold, together with the cover itself, and they must face each other; i.e. both types of *mitzvos* must be fulfilled in harmony. Only then will Hashem meet us, and let us hear His Voice.

Israel's worship of the Golden Calf was a transgression of a command from *one* of the two Tablets. Why then did Moshe Rabbeinu smash *both* of them? The answer is that the Ten Commandments are not multiple choice — one Tablet cannot exist without the other intact.

Have you ever met a religious Jew who was dishonest in his business? Never. Because, by definition, an unethical person cannot be "religious." There does exist a phenomenon we could call "cultural Orthodoxy," keeping some *mitzvos* to conform with one's peer group, without any accompanying commitment. Jewish pickpockets in old Warsaw all spoke Yiddish, all had beards, and all kept Shabbos! Just as Yiddish was the only language they knew, and just as every man had a beard, so too did everyone keep Shabbos; that was their life-style. It was a good thing; but it has little to do with relating to Hashem.

These ideas are very well known, though it pays to repeat them now and then. However, the reverse is much less well known, and that is: Just as fulfillment of the *mitzvos* between human beings is absolutely necessary to give meaning to our relationship with Hashem, so too, a meaningful relationship with Hashem is absolutely necessary to give meaning to the *mitzvos* between human beings. If the first Tablet, the *mitzvah* against idolatry, is broken, then the second Tablet must also be destroyed. That requires explanation.

We have all met good people who are not observant Jews or who are not Jewish at all. Why should we say that kindness and honesty are contingent on fulfilling *mitzvos* between us and Hashem? Indeed, it says, *Kindness performed by the nations of the world is basically sinful* (*Proverbs* 14:34). How can this be?

Nowadays, we are so happy when anyone does a *mitzvah* that we pay little attention to what their reason for doing it might be. Do you come to *shul* or pledge *tzedakah* out of habit, or guilt feelings, or a desire for honor? We don't mind. We're glad to have you with us, and our charitable organization will cheerfully accept your money. But those who dig deeper, those who get to explore advanced-level *Yiddishkeit,* begin to discover that there are many secrets of emotion and motivation hidden behind a good deed. Those who search the darker corners of the soul might sometimes even find themselves agreeing with the poet who wrote, "the last temptation is the greatest treason; to do the right deed for the wrong reason." Sometimes.

A slain American civil rights leader was famous not only for leadership, but also for his selfless love; so selfless that he refused to let his wife and child derive any personal benefit from the civil rights movement. Without questioning his sincerity, we can still ask: Did that selflessness truly have its source in the man's honesty and love for his people? Or was his relationship with his wife tainted as a result of his many infidelities, revealed after his death by admiring biographers?

The human soul is complex, and very deep. We never understand any person completely, nor are we meant to. But one thing we do know: Virtually all people spend nearly every waking minute thinking about themselves.

The murder of a child in Jerusalem or half a dozen students in California does not concern us as much as a pain in our little finger. This does not mean we are wicked, it is simply the human condition. Because of this, a prominent psychiatrist pointed out that much of what appears to be kindness is really a form of psychological game-playing. Someone may offer help in order to impress others with his philanthropy, to atone for a guilty conscience, to compensate for feelings of inferiority, to make others feel inferior that they need his help, or for a hundred other reasons all bound up with personal ego. That is not *chesed*, the kindness of the Torah.

Chesed, true human relationships, are tied to spiritual intimacy; when you are able to step outside yourself, to seriously feel for another person, and to feel connected *to* that person. If the link is there, if you have that warmth of feeling, then there is a natural desire to *want* to make them happy, and to help them, as natural as the desire to give joy to one's own children.

How do we learn to step outside ourselves? What will make us feel that connection with others? The only way to accomplish this is by strengthening our link with Hashem.

To perceive the Creator in our lives is to recognize how small we all are, tiny specks of creation, each one totally insignificant. Except that each of us, all of us, are also bound *to* the Creator, all of us have the glory of being His servants and His children. That bond, the perception that we have meaning only through Hashem and that all of us share this same essence of meaning, is what allows us to leave the prison of ego and to feel for one another and to want to share whatever blessings we possess.

As the Midrash says, anyone with *yiras Shamayim*, true reverence for Heaven, will also have in him *chesed*, true kindness. The Midrash continues, anyone with *chesed* will also have *yiras Shamayim*. They are inseparable, two angels fashioned from the same block of gold, both coming forth from the cover of the *Aron Kodesh*.

A man wanted to convert to Judaism, but only if he could learn the entire Torah while standing on one foot. Hillel said, "What is hateful to you, do not do to your friend; that is the whole Torah." Rashi explains: Half the Torah is learning to relate to our friends. The other half is learning that *HaKadosh Baruch Hu* is the closest friend of all.

If we begin sincerely, from *either* side of the *Aron Kodesh*, we will surely end up at the other. When we have both together, the two angels facing each other, it is then that Hashem says He will meet with us and speak with us, and it is then that we will truly understand what it is He is coming to say.

Vayikra:
Having It All

The *mitzvah* of *korbanos*, sacrificial offerings, is introduced with the words: *Adam ki yakriv mikem korban, Any person among you who shall bring an offering* (*Leviticus* 1:2). The Torah could have written more briefly: *Ki yakriv mikem, Anyone among you*. Why the extra word *Adam?*

The Midrash says this word *Adam* is a hint to us. A literal translation of *Adam* is Adam, the first human being. This is to teach us: "Offerings Adam brought to Hashem were surely not stolen, because the whole world belonged to him. Just as Adam's offerings were honestly acquired, so too should all your offerings be honestly acquired, and not be brought from anything stolen."

There are people who would never dream of defrauding anyone to benefit themselves, but who stretch *halachah* to raise funds for *tzedakah* because "a *mitzvah* is different." They could not be more wrong, because someone who steals for the sake of a *mitzvah* is, in effect, making the Almighty an accomplice in crime. So from the very beginning the Torah warns us, offerings are desired only if acquired without sin.

Important as this lesson is, it is strange that the Torah teaches it by referring to Adam: Just as *he* was honest because everything belonged to him, so too should we be honest. Why doesn't it simply say, "Don't steal even for a *mitzvah*," without alluding to the first man?

Perhaps the reason is: Besides the commandment, the Torah is also teaching us an attitude; *how to cope* with the human desire to acquire more and more, by legal means or otherwise, and the chronic envy of whatever others possess. The Torah tells us: Look at Adam. He had no financial insecurity, no temptation to steal, because the entire world was his. In the same way, we can also handle *our* insecurity, and our temptation, if we only recognize the profound truth: The entire world is ours.

As our Sages put it: Every person is obligated to say, "For me was the universe created!" That is not conceit. It is a perception of the reality that the Creator planned His world with each of us in mind, and that everything around you was put there by Him to help *you* fulfill the mission on earth for which you were made.

Your family, your in-laws, your co-workers, your health, your material possessions and also whatever luxuries you do *not* possess — what we have was given to us by Hashem because He knows it is the best possible situation for us, right now. We may not understand why, and it is proper to try to improve our lot in ways approved by the Torah. But as long as we are where we are, we need to know: This is where Hashem put me, and He has surely given me everything I truly need.

If you do not own a wheelchair, crutches, or medicine for ulcers or heart disease, that is no reason to feel jealous of those who do. Hashem has blessed you that you don't need those things. And if you know that Hashem made the whole world for you, and for some reason He did not choose to give you a certain kind of home or car or stock portfolio, it is also not a reason to feel upset. It just means that at least for now, to do what *you* need to do on earth, those are encumbrances you don't presently need.

Simple-minded people think that success is measured by the things we possess, as if life is a game and "he who dies with the most toys wins." But a book for corporate executives points out: Ultimate success is when you are no longer burdened with "things." An expensive briefcase is a status symbol; but the corporation president carries no briefcase at all, because his importance is in the ideas of his head. The rising young executive wears a certain brand of gold watch; but David Rockefeller wore *no* watch, because he did not worry about being late, nothing important happened at meetings until he arrived. The ultimate success symbol is to carry no money, because the restaurant's *maitre d'* knows you, and sends the bill to corporate headquarters without you even having to *look* at it.

That is a true *mashal*, an analogy to the life of a *tzaddik*. He has no special desire to possess more "things"; and in his knowledge that Hashem made the world for *him*, he enjoys the beauty of luxuries even if they "belong" to others. On Pesach night it is a *mitzvah* to celebrate by putting out silver, if you have any. The great *Maharil* once had some silver which belonged to a non-Jew, and Pesach night he put it out on display. It gave him just as much pleasure because he understood that Hashem made it for *him* to enjoy.

When you see a beautiful home, an attractive garden, or expensive furniture, enjoy the sight. The owners have already become used to it, and very likely it no longer brings them joy. But you, like Adam — recognizing that the world is made for your benefit and beauty is created to give you pleasure — can enjoy it, and thank Hashem for it; and then you can return home, to enjoy your own possessions just as well.

The approach of this *sidrah* means that the month of Nissan is upon us, a time for celebrating freedom; but freedom is meaningful only if we can use it to get what we want from life. And, as a *tzaddik* once said, "The only way to get what you want is to want whatever it is you get!" By remembering Adam, and that we, his children, have also been given a world custom made for us, we can come to enjoy what we have, and what others have; and also to come to enjoy the very *presence* of other people, knowing that Hashem made them in order to add something special to our lives; and that He made us to add something special to theirs.

Tazria: Unified Diversity

A male child is to be circumcised on the eighth day. *Bris milah* may never be performed before eight days, and may not be delayed beyond eight days if it is possible to do so at the proper time. This *mitzvah* is already recorded in detail in the Book of Genesis, and the Rabbis explain that it is repeated here to teach that *bris milah* is performed on the eighth day even if that day is Shabbos. Causing a wound is normally forbidden on Shabbos, so the Torah comes to tell us that the *mitzvah* of *milah* in its proper time is an exception to the rule.

The Sages of the Gemara differ as to how far this exception extends. Rabbi Eliezer ruled that the Torah is permitting not only the act of circumcision, but also any necessary preparations to be performed on Shabbos. One could buy the required bandages on Shabbos and could even sharpen the *milah* knife. The majority of the Sages disagree with Rabbi Eliezer, permitting only the circumcision itself, while other preparations must all be made in advance. The *halachah* follows the majority, and therefore all preparations for a Shabbos *bris* must be done in advance.

A number of years passed before this *halachah* was finally decided, and in the interim there was a town which followed Rabbi Eliezer's lenient opinion, which they were entitled to do. Their *mitzvah* enthusiasm was so great that when it once happened that the *milah* knife was missing, they chopped down a tree and burned the wood to make charcoal, in order to heat up metal to fashion a new knife — all on Shabbos. The Gemara says that because of their love for the *mitzvah*, the townspeople were rewarded with special Divine protection from the Romans, and they all lived to a ripe old age.

But Rav Moshe Feinstein z.l. asked, why were they rewarded? The final *halachah* is that it is *forbidden* to violate Shabbos for *bris milah* preparation, and what they did is considered Shabbos desecration. They are not to be blamed for relying on Rabbi Eliezer, but since we now know Rabbi Eliezer was wrong, why did Heaven reward them?

Rav Moshe answered: We see from here that it is not always our job to determine "absolute" truth. Flesh and blood cannot always know what absolute truth is. Instead, our job is to do what Hashem desires of us; and it is His desire that we follow the *halachah* according to the Torah authorities we have. If someday we discover an error, even if the *halachah* would change, we have nevertheless fulfilled our *mitzvah* in the meantime, and Hashem will reward us for it.

This involves a fine distinction. We must not deviate from *halachah* by a hair. But at the same time, it is possible for *more* than one *halachah* to exist, and each community must follow

Tazria: Unified Diversity

its own authorities. Of course, this applies only to when the disagreement is between legitimate Torah authorities; non-Orthodox clergy who do not accept the Torah's divinity are by definition not included in this. But within the Torah camp, legitimate differences of opinion in *halachah* and *hashkafah* (Torah outlook) do exist, and we are commanded and rewarded for fidelity to our own authentic leadership.

A noteworthy illustration of this "unity in diversity" is the observance of the *sefirah* period between Pesach and Shavuos, when we refrain from weddings, haircuts and listening to music. We do this to commemorate the twenty-four-thousand disciples of Rabbi Akiva who died in a plague, whom the Talmud says perished for the sin of not treating one another with sufficient respect. Part of *sefirah* observance is to recall that ethical failure, to act with extra *derech eretz* among ourselves, and to strengthen our feelings of Jewish unity; which makes it all very strange when you consider that there is a three-way controversy concerning just when *sefirah* is.

Many Jews practice *sefirah* restrictions from Pesach until Lag B'Omer, and then cease. Others do not begin the restrictions until a week after Pesach on Rosh Chodesh Iyar, and they continue the mourning period until Shavuos. A third group begins at Pesach and goes all the way to Shavuos, but eases the restrictions on Rosh Chodesh Iyar, Rosh Chodesh Sivan and Lag B'Omer. This is perhaps the only *mitzvah* in which there are different opinions in the calendar itself *when* the days of observance fall. Isn't that a bizarre way to strengthen Jewish unity?

Obviously, this itself *is* the lesson of unity. *Halachah* sets the standard, the only standard there is. But when there are different authoritative opinions in defining a *halachah*, then each loyal Jew follows his or her teachers or community or family custom. That is the true *derech eretz,* the respect of one another which recognizes that the one Torah will guide a number of people in a number of different ways, each of which is the Will of Hashem for that individual Jew.

(The above was originally delivered as a Shabbos morning *devar Torah*, at a time when news from *Eretz Yisrael* was not very optimistic. Some additional remarks which were made then are still appropriate, and they follow below.)

As you know, the tangled world of Middle East politics has seen a Rogers peace plan, a Reagan peace plan, an Allon plan, a Schultz plan, a Baker plan and others — none of which have worked; so let me take the liberty of offering one of my own.

Sefarim tell us that the harmony, or the animosity, between Jew and gentile to a great degree reflects the state of harmony between Jew and Jew. As the Talmud says, the Romans were able to destroy Jerusalem only when Jerusalem's Jews began attacking one another. If the Jews in *Eretz Yisrael* could only have harmony among themselves, that would set off a spiritual chain-reaction, which *HaKadosh Baruch Hu* would use to create peace in the Middle East.

We do not expect to see that Jewish harmony in *Eretz Yisrael* in the near future, especially with the unfortunate secular-religious conflict so embedded in the Israeli social fabric. However, it is reasonable to suggest that the state of harmony between observant and non-observant Jews is itself a spiritual reflection, a mirror image of the degree of harmony among observant Jews themselves. If all *Torah* Jews would be united, that would create a chain reaction of sanctity to impact on the secular-religious equation, which would then have a ripple effect on peace between Jew and Arab.

Perhaps you believe that harmony among observant Jews is as much a pipe dream as harmony between Jews and Arabs? Granted. However, the reason why Jewish unity has such an effect on Jewish-gentile relations is because Divine spiritual power is concentrated only in those people who truly understand. Hashem made His world in such a way that the people who know Him, and who know that their actions affect the world, are the ones whose unity or lack of it affects others. That is why only internal Jewish harmony has a ripple effect, because gentiles don't know the principle; and that is why harmony among observant Jews is necessary, because secular

Jews don't know about this any more than gentiles do. My hypothesis therefore is:

If *shalom*, the state of peace in the world, depends on the state of *shalom* among those who recognize the spiritual dynamics of the world, then to create this chain reaction you need not begin with *all* Jews, and not even with all observant Jews. You need only begin by creating true *shalom* within the small group of Jews who *do* understand, those who realize that their *shalom does* echo through the world. That alone is enough, because if indeed only they comprehend, then the source of the Divine power for peace is concentrated in them.

This may sound outlandishly mystical to some people, but certainly it is no more outlandish than the ideas of Schultz, Reagan, Allon, etc., and it has a basis in Torah tradition. If we would begin with one group, with the people who comprehend the *parashah* of *bris milah* and its lesson, and if we would make extra efforts to create harmony, *shalom* and *derech eretz* among ourselves, even just from now to Shavuos, that alone would surely have an effect.

After Rabbi Akiva's disciples died, he rebuilt the Torah foundation of the Jewish nation with only five new students. Five are enough. And if five, ten, or fifty of us would do all we can to try to feel love for those around us, and compassion, and a desire to treat others with respect; who knows what the ripple effect might be, all the way to the Middle East? And if not that far, at the very least it would have a beneficial effect on us, and on those around us, until Shavuos, and beyond.

Metzora:
The Dangers
of Being Human

A major figure in this *sidrah* is the *metzora*, a man or woman afflicted with the illness called *tzara'as*. *Tzara'as* is often translated as leprosy, but the evidence demonstrates that this translation is not correct. The *metzora* must live outside the city, but if the disease spreads over his entire body he may return home, which would surely not be permitted if we are dealing with laws of quarantine of contagious disease. From this and other evidence, commentators conclude that *tzara'as* was a supernatural phenomenon, sent by Heaven as punishment for sin. We do not have *tzara'as* today because we are no longer on the spiritual level to deserve the Divine message, and in our sorry state, we would always be sick.

Tradition teaches that the chief cause of *tzara'as*, the true disease of which lesions of the skin was only the symptom, was the sin of slander. The Gemara says that the word *metzora* itself stands for *motzi-[shem-] ra*, a spreader of malicious gossip. The Torah therefore sends the *metzora* out of the camp, as the Midrash explains: "He created ill will and enmity among people; let him live alone, away from other people entirely." Just as the illness is spiritual, so too is the cure. When he does *teshuvah*, and Heaven sees his sincere repentance, the disease disappears and he returns to society.

Upon his return, he brings an offering. *This is the law of the metzora on the day he becomes purified, and he shall be brought to the Kohen* (*Leviticus* 14:2). What is the meaning of "he shall be *brought*?" Let it say, "he shall *come*." The Midrash answers: to teach us that he should not delay. Even if he does not want to come, let him be brought, he *must* return.

This requires explanation. The *metzora*, afflicted with a terrible disease, also suffered the punishment of having to leave his home and live alone outside the camp. He learned his lesson, repented, and is now finally able to return. Why would anyone delay? And why must the Torah give a special warning *not* to delay?

Perhaps the answer is: Divine punishment is not vengeance. More often, it is a form of therapy, to awaken the sinner to his own spiritual self. The *metzora* is banished from the city not as retribution, but as moral instruction: "You look down on others, and continually speak ill of them? Then leave the city, spend your days in solitary confinement until you ache for companionship; until you learn how beautiful is the sound of a human voice, anyone's voice, and how fortunate we are to have others with whom to share the world. When you learn that lesson, Hashem will heal your body, because by then you yourself will have healed your soul."

However, this therapy has its risks. The *metzora* might well decide: "In society, I sinned. Perhaps it is better that I continue to remain alone?" People released from prison sometimes commit crimes to be reincarcerated, just as some refugees from the Soviet Union returned there; because it is sometimes easier *not* to be free, easier not to have to make decisions for oneself. The *metzora* in his solitary meditations might conclude: Why do I need the trouble of human relations, of getting along with spouse and in-laws and neighbors? Better to live in a cave, without possibility of gossip, it is safer that way.

But the Torah says that he's wrong. Cave-dwelling may be safer, but it is not better. Had Hashem desired that we refrain from slander by avoiding all conversation, he could have commanded us to Scotch-tape our mouths or to cut out our tongues. The purpose of life is that we are put here to interact *with* others and with the world around us, and to do so with *kiddush Hashem,* sanctifying the Name of our Creator with our speech and deeds.

Sometimes, emergency measures are required, and the potential sociopath who has lost his feeling for others is sent outside the camp to recover. But once he regains his perspective, he is commanded that on the day he becomes purified, he must be brought to the *Kohen* without delay; he must return to live in society, with all its dangers, because only within human society can human beings be fully alive.

We no longer have *tzara'as*, but the lessons still need to be learned. To learn not to speak ill of other people, because we *need* them, because every person adds something to our lives. And also to learn that Hashem does not want us to live alone in a cave, not even in a cave created by our own emotions. Many people walk around encased in a protective shell, wearing a sign that says: Do not touch. It is as if they were afraid of coming close, afraid of being hurt by human intimacy. And is it not a great sadness that the very word "intimacy" has become almost extinct except in an erotic sense?

He must be *brought*, one who can participate in human relations must participate. This does not mean you should be part of every poker game and cocktail party, and it does not mean you must socialize with people who belittle you. But you do have work to do, to work to develop the feeling that these people around you are *your* people; you are part *of* them and feel comfortable *with* them; because this is the place where G-d has sent you and the place where you truly belong.

Kedoshim: Grudge-Bearing

Do not take revenge nor bear a grudge against your people, but you shall love your neighbor as yourself; I am Hashem (Leviticus 19:18).

One might wonder why the Torah placed the commandment of love together with the prohibition against revenge or bearing a grudge. Why not be itself, as an introduction to all the *mitzvos* between one Jew and another; or together with a more "loving" commandment, like charity, ransoming captives or kindness to a spouse? Perhaps the Torah is emphasizing that we must love even when it is most difficult to do so. But if so, the *mitzvah* should appear together with the prohibition against hatred. What is the special relationship between love and not bearing a grudge which ties these two *mitzvos* together?

There is a true story, which took place over a century ago in a small town in Eastern Europe. The hero of the story was the town rabbi, whose name I have forgotten. But the name of the villain was Grunem ben Getzel, called Gruntzy for short. Gruntzy was a *moser*, a Jewish informer. He was friendly with the local chief of police, and Gruntzy would threaten to expose the real or imagined crimes of the local Jewish community unless the community paid him a monthly stipend as protection money. Gruntzy was universally loathed, but there was nothing the townspeople could do to him.

The time came when the town elected a new rabbi, a *tzaddik* who was courageously honest, and who also refused to listen to gossip. The townspeople decided: "Better not tell the Rav about Gruntzy. What he doesn't know won't hurt him, and it might be safer for all of us."

One market day, a Jewish farmer from an outlying district brought his produce to town to sell, and he set up his little stand early in the morning. Gruntzy passed by on his way to *shul* — in those days, even criminals went to *minyan* — and Gruntzy selected a basketful of the choicest fruits and vegetables, and walked off without paying. The simple farmer was too dumbfounded to speak, and he decided that his customer must be absent minded, and he would remind him at the *minyan*.

After *shacharis*, the farmer approached Gruntzy: "Excuse me, Reb Yid, but you forgot to pay me for the produce." Gruntzy replied, "Pay? Gruntzy never pays" — and he left. The flabbergasted farmer shouted, "Where is the Rav?" (The rabbi in those times was also the local Jewish court.) The townspeople tried to dissuade the indignant farmer, but he stormed over to the rabbi's house, told his story, and the rabbi sent the *shammas* to fetch Gruntzy.

The *shammas* did not want to go, but in those days the *shammas* had to listen to the rabbi, so he went. He returned with the message that Gruntzy refused to appear and was also very angry. That Shabbos morning, Gruntzy told the *shul's gabbai* that he wanted to be called to the Torah for *shlishi*, the rabbi's *aliyah*, to put the Rav in his place. The frightened *gabbai* complied, and called him up. As Gruntzy proudly approached the *bimah*, the rabbi walked over and slapped him across his face. Gruntzy turned red, and left the *shul*. The congregants were terrified, but the rabbi remained calm, and *davening* continued as usual.

A few days later, the rabbi and the *shammas* were walking on the road to attend a *bris* at a nearby village, when suddenly they saw several Russian soldiers coming towards them, led by Gruntzy with a drawn sword. The *shammas* said, "*Shema Yisrael*"; but the rabbi just looked calmly at Gruntzy. They faced each other for a long moment; and then Gruntzy dropped his sword and ran off.

The astonished *shammas* asked: "Rebbi, a miracle! How did you do it?"

The rabbi explained: "It is written, *Just as water reflects whatever expression you put on your face, so too, another man's heart will reflect whatever emotion you feel in your own* (*Proverbs* 27:19). The whole town hates Gruntzy, which caused him to reciprocate, with hatred and more hatred growing ever more bitter. But I refused to become part of it. Even when I slapped Gruntzy, my thoughts were only for his benefit. And now, I faced him with the love of knowing that he still remains a child of Avraham, Yitzchak and Yaakov, come what may. The thoughts in my heart created an echo, or a reflection, in his. It broke the cycle and he threw down his sword."

The Torah describes a dispute between the shepherds of Avraham and the shepherds of Lot: *The land could not bear them that they might live together, for their property was great, and they could not live together* (*Genesis* 13:16). Rav Meir Simcha of Dvinsk pointed out that the Torah repeats itself: The land could not bear them to live together, for their property was great; and they could not live together. Why say it twice?

Rav Meir Simcha answered: The original cause of the dispute, *why* they could not live together, was because their property was so great. But once any dispute begins, it takes on a life of its own, feeding on itself, and the original reason becomes irrelevant. They could not live together, because of the property; but after the argument got going, they could not live together, period.

And perhaps this explains why the Torah juxtaposes (in *Leviticus* 18:19) *Love your neighbor* with *Do not bear a grudge.* In most social *mitzvos* — charity, honesty, displays of respect — even if there is not a feeling of love, the *mitzvah* can be viable. But when there is a lust for vengeance, or a well-nursed grudge, that is already an emotional reaction to the deeds of the other person. There has already been created an echo, a reflection of feeling; like water reflects a face, so does one heart affect another. The cycle has begun, and we are caught in a trap.

Therefore, it is here that the Torah commands: *Love your neighbor as yourself* (*Leviticus* 19:18). Break the cycle, short-circuit the wiring by consciously asserting a feeling of love to someone who has caused you pain. Not for *his* sake, but for your own, to escape from that destructive pattern which causes spiritual ulcers, and sometimes physical ulcers as well.

Some commentaries write that *Love your neighbor as yourself* cannot be meant literally, because it is impossible. If so, we might suggest that the Torah is hinting to us that *Love your neighbor as yourself* includes, "Love him *because* you love yourself"; because you know that if you do not assert feelings of love, you will inevitably wither away in bitterness and self-pity.

Even if you are not sentimental by nature, it is possible to develop the emotion with training and exercise. To look at another Jew and whisper: "That is someone Hashem loves, someone with holiness, and someone who is eternally bonded to me by their soul — I love you." Even if it sounds trite at first, in time the feeling will come. If we begin by practicing on people we already like, after a while we can move on to others, to encompass more and more of Hashem's people in our emotional circle, growing greater as we make others part of our spiritual selves.

Emor: Temporary Elevations

We are no longer able to fulfill the *mitzvos* of *korbanos*, sacrificial offerings; but since they are written in the Torah for every generation to study, it means they have lessons to teach every generation and for every person to apply each day. One of these lessons is the *mitzvah* in this *sidrah* (*Leviticus* 22:21) that offerings must be unblemished, without injury or disease. A *korban* symbolizes our desire to honor Hashem, and if we cannot afford an expensive gift, whatever we *do* offer should be perfect without defects.

Gentiles are also permitted to bring offerings to the *Beis HaMikdash*, and many of them did. The Torah therefore commands: *Also from a stranger, a non-Jew, do not sacrifice any of these defective animals* (*ibid*. v. 25). One may wonder, the Gemara says that non-Jews are permitted to bring blemished animals on their private altars; why does the Torah ordain here that gentile offerings have the same law as those of Jews?

The answer is that gentiles may indeed offer blemished animals, but only if the offering is one brought outside the Sanctuary. If the president of the United States wishes to sacrifice to Hashem in the White House Rose Garden, a defective animal is also acceptable. But at the Sanctuary, at the *Beis HaMikdash*, even a pagan must conform to the higher standard of bringing offerings without any blemish.

We see here an illustration of a general principle. The Creator judges each of us according to our abilities, and he accepts our individual limitations; not only physical and financial limitations, but even emotional ones. The gentile has the same financial capability to purchase a perfect animal that a Jew does. But Hashem, knowing it is too much to ask of the average pagan, therefore accepts even the diseased or injured bull brought by the non-Jew.

However, this is true only when the non-Jew is in his own home. When he visits the House of Hashem, when he enters the *Mikdash*, then the Torah commands him: In a Holy Place, you too can rise to holiness. At least for this moment, at least while you are here, you can raise your sights and jump to a higher level. For a few minutes, every person can make the effort to transcend his or her limitations to enter a different world, Hashem's world, the world of perfection. And then, even when you leave, and you return to pagan society, something of this experience will accompany you, and some memory of the higher life will remain.

You may ask: May I avoid this "higher" experience? May I remain comfortably within my own limitations by not visiting the Sanctuary? The answer is: Yes, you may, if you are not Jewish. But Jews *are* obligated to visit, we are commanded to come, and to rise above ourselves, at least some of the time. You are commanded to explore, and to surprise yourself by discovering spiritual strength you did not know you possessed; and then to take some of it home with you, for everyday use.

To choose a couple of simple examples: Many people in *shul* are afraid to let themselves go, to *daven* more slowly or loudly, or even to answer a boisterous *amen*; as if, Heaven forbid, they might discover that *davening* can be enjoyable or that they themselves are more "religious" than they had suspected. Many of us shy away from extending a "Good Morning" or a "Good Shabbos" to people we don't know well, even if we share the same *shul* or street or just the same Father in Heaven (doesn't that make us related enough to greet one another with a smile?).

At the turn of the twentieth century, a Jewish child in Poland was kidnaped and raised as a Catholic. Sixty years later, by a miracle of *hashgachah pratis,* Divine providence, she was reunited with her family. She remembered nothing of her childhood, and thought of herself as a Polish Catholic. But when she attended a Pesach *Seder,* she suddenly found herself reading the *Haggadah*, in Hebrew! — until they pointed out to her that she was doing it, and her memory went blank once more. In the same way, we are so trapped by our own self-images that we are not *so* pious, not so *frum* and kind and loving, that our self-imposed limitations do not allow the inner sanctity to even show itself.

Perhaps the way for most of us to escape from the spiritual rut is what the psychiatrist told a patient who had nothing organically wrong, but whose arm was totally paralyzed. He would not move a muscle. But when the psychiatrist asked him to describe how his arm *used* to be, the man said: "I used to have perfect control. I could move my arm this way and that" — and he demonstrated by *freely swinging the afflicted arm* — "but now I cannot move it at all."

If for a moment we can only forget what we are, or what we think we are, and try to imagine the righteous, saintly person we theoretically could be, we can create a mental picture, to enjoy for a moment. And then perhaps we will discover that pictures can become animated, and that spiritual paralysis is not so permanent, after all.

An ideal place to begin is in *shul*. Just as *korbanos* symbolize the devotion to Hashem we desire to feel, so too when we visit the *mikdash m'at,* the miniature Sanctuary or our own synagogue, it is a time to strive as best we can to act and feel sanctified, without blemish. At least for a moment, we can pause to try to imagine what a true *tzaddik* must be like, and to imagine the love a *tzaddik* feels towards people who are around him. We can role-play, stretching our minds to feel what sanctity might be, at least for the short time we are in this holy place.

And then, having entered a place of holiness both physically and mentally, we can try to take a little bit of the holiness home. By doing our best to set aside a short time for sincere prayer, reverence and sharing of love in the Sanctuary, we will find that when we leave, the Sanctuary goes with us; improving our lives in our families and schools and workplaces, adding also to them that same sense of Divine reverence, sharing and love.

Bamidbar: Choosing a Team

The *sidrah* includes the special *mitzvah* of *degalim*, flags or signs, a commandment that the twelve tribes are to encamp and march through the wilderness in a particular order. Yehudah is to be on the east, and next to him is Yissachar followed by Zevulun. On the south is Reuven adjacent to Shimon and then Gad, and so on for all the tribes. Anyone who has ever had to arrange seating for a large group knows the need for planning and order. But why did Hashem have to provide Moshe Rabbeinu with a detailed seating plan? Couldn't Moshe conceive a plan of his own?

Perhaps the reason for this is some secret beyond human comprehension; but the Midrash says that the impact of this arrangement was quite visible to human beings. The Midrash asks: After Pharaoh set Israel free, why did he change his mind and pursue us? Our rabbis answer that Egypt thought their Israelite slaves were of little value. But when they saw our fathers encamped in the order of their banners, the *degalim*, Egypt said, *Vay!* Why did we allow such precious people to escape?

This order is inscribed in the Torah for all time, which means it is important for us even today. Rashi quotes a midrash that the arrangement was first set up by our father Yaakov. Yaakov told his children the precise order in which to march at his own funeral, and Hashem agreed: This is the order, forever. But what is so eternally important about who stands next to whom?

It is a well-known principle that to succeed in Torah, one must become part of the *klal*, the Torah community. Nine Rabbi Akivas cannot say a *kaddish,* but ten ordinary Jews can. However holy we may be, we cannot fully relate to Hashem without others; and the Gemara says that a Jew who refuses to join the community cuts himself off from eternity, because the eternal reward of *Olam Haba* is only for those who are part of *Klal Yisrael.*

We know all this; but here the Torah reveals something more. Not only is teamwork important, but different people belong on *different* teams, and part of success is finding the team where *you* work best.

For example, the Gemara says that one may not leave *Eretz Yisrael* except in certain special circumstances, one of which is in order to study Torah. What if *Eretz Yisrael* has its own *yeshivos;* may one still leave to study Torah in a foreign land? The answer is that one may. The reason for this, the Gemara explains, is that even the most outstanding teacher may not be the best for this particular student; and with all the *yeshivos* in Jerusalem and Bnei Brak, it is possible that *this* boy must go elsewhere to find the rebbe who can best relate to him.

Rav Eliyahu Lopian was one of the great Torah giants of the last generation, and a famous teacher in *Eretz Yisrael* in the 1950's and 60's. But in the 1940's, when Rav Lopian was teaching in England, he was relatively unknown and unsuccessful, while other Torah leaders in England during that period became famous. Each person has a specific social environment where his or her soul can thrive, and it is a special blessing to be able to discover those people who can help make it happen.

Even in regard to our ultimate redemption, the prophecy is: *Mashiach* will come from the family of Yehudah; but for *Mashiach* to succeed, he must also receive help from a righteous hero of the family of Yosef, Mashiach ben Yosef. Even the Messiah cannot be victorious unless he is part of a team, and it must be the particular team in which each one's ability complements the abilities of others.

This is the meaning of the Divinely ordained plan for the Israelite camp in the wilderness, where Hashem followed the prophetic arrangement made by our father Yaakov. The greatness of the tribe of Yissachar, the full flowering of this talent, can only blossom when he stands between Yehudah and Zevulun. Shimon will shine most brightly in serving *Klal Yisrael,* if Reuven is next to him, with Gad on the other side; and so on for each of the twelve tribes, each one affecting and being affected in turn.

It is worthwhile to try to discover why each tribe was assigned its particular position; why Yissachar, for instance, worked best when influenced by Zevulun and Yehudah. But the general principle for us is clear: To realize our full spiritual potential, we must have an opportunity to work with those people who are most spiritually compatible with out particular souls.

Surely this is one reason why *HaKadosh Baruch Hu* arranged for the existence of *Ashkenazim* and *Sefardim, Chassidim* and non-*Chassidim,* and other groups, so that each individual can find kindred spirits with whom to serve Hashem in ways most suited to him or her.

It also explains why the Gemara says Hashem spends His day making *shidduchim*, matching up the right man and woman to become husband and wife. Why do we need Hashem for this; can't we choose our own spouses? Since marriage is a spiritual bonding of two people, only Hashem knows which souls are truly compatible, which personalities can grow together in soul; and therefore we need Him to bring together the right man and woman, at the right time.

Ideally, we should have a prophet to reveal the workings of our individual souls, showing us what sort of people are best for us to work with. No longer possessing prophecy, we must resort to trial and error. But it is therefore all the more imperative to avoid the mistake of thinking that a spiritual failure indicates that you don't have what it takes.

Some people who go through the tragedy of divorce conclude that marriage is not for them, ever. But if one is halachically permitted to remarry, that conclusion is usually a mistake. Even if you ended up with the wrong spouse, that doesn't mean marriage in general is not for you; and by refusing to remarry, one might be depriving that unknown person who was created by Heaven as your perfect partner, and who will wait out his or her life without ever knowing who you are.

Another area where finding the right team is especially crucial is in working for community institutions like *yeshivos, shuls* and *tzedakah* groups. We must all work for the community, not only because we are needed, but also because our own spiritual development is incomplete until we are a full part of Hashem's congregation. But many people *do* get involved, and then something happens to turn them off: a disappointment, a personality clash, a lack of enjoyment; and they withdraw from active service, to sit quietly on the sidelines (or sometimes not so quietly).

But since community service is an essential part of *Yiddishkeit*, it follows that it is possible for everyone to find a way to serve which is fulfilling and a source of happiness. Those who have not yet found a way or who have been disappointed in the past should therefore consider the possibility that the team they were on was perhaps not the team best suited to them, and look for another. Each new group of people is a new combination of personalities and souls, which means there are new opportunities for everyone to join in, opportunities which were not available before.

This *sidrah* is read around Shavuos time, the time when our ancestors said נַעֲשֶׂה וְנִשְׁמָע, *we will keep the Torah and we will listen* (*Exodus* 24:7) — we, all together. And Shavuos is a good time to approach the directors of your *shul* or *yeshivah* to ask: What can *I* do, how can *I* take part? Not only to help out, but to help discover a new dimension in myself, to see how I interact with this particular group, with this particular kind of holiness. With that attitude, all the families of *Klal Yisrael* will work together in the Divine arrangement, encamped as one around the *Aron Kodesh,* and marching as one, until together we reach the promised land.

Beha'alosecha: Teaching

At the beginning of *Parashas Beha'alosecha,* the *Kohen* is given the *mitzvah* to light the *menorah* in the Sanctuary of the *Mishkan*. The word used for lighting, *beha'alosecha*, literally means "when you lift up," implying elevation. *Rashi* explains that this word was chosen to hint to us two *halachos*, two laws pertaining to lighting. One is that when putting the match to the wick, do not take your hand away until the flame is burning strongly by itself, to teach us that the flame must be lifted, it must rise on its own.

The second *halachah* which is hinted at is that it was required to place a small platform in front of the *menorah*, a step "lifted up" off the ground, on which the *Kohen* stood while preparing the wicks for lighting each day. Rav Moshe Feinstein *z.l.* noted that it is odd for one word in the Torah to teach two such different *halachos*, to light until the candle burns alone, and also to stand on a step; and there must therefore be some connection between these two requirements.

Perhaps we can suggest that the connection is found in the teaching of our Sages that the *menorah* symbolizes the light of Torah knowledge. We are told to hold the match until the candle burns brightly on its own, and, in addition to its plain meaning, this is also a message to every parent and teacher: It is not enough to give a lesson for the student to parrot back mechanically. The goal must be to light a flame which will burn "by itself," to create a fire in the students, such a love of learning that they continue to make progress on their own, long after the teacher is gone.

But how does the teacher light the fire? How do we inspire students to want to achieve? The Torah offers a first step in that same word, *beha'alosecha,* teaching us that we also need a *ma'alah,* an elevated platform. Why? The *menorah* was not so tall. A *Kohen* could clean and light it while standing on the ground. But the reason for the elevation was that without it, although the basic lamplighting job could be performed, one would not be standing high enough to be able to look down *into* the interior of the lamp itself. You can still wipe out excess oil, and insert a new wick. But without a step up to look down into the *menorah*, you cannot see exactly what needs to be done to clean it thoroughly, and to ensure that today's candle will burn its very brightest.

There are professional teachers who are experts at preparing lesson-plans. But one cannot touch a child's soul, one cannot kindle a flame which will burn on its own, until one climbs *up* and looks *into* the child; trying to understand who is this particular boy or girl, what are the child's needs, what residue from yesterday is interfering with progress today, and how we can prepare that boy or girl's emotional candle to make it burn most brightly for that child.

One word in the Torah teaches two lessons, because the two are interconnected. The aim of true education is to make the child into a self-starter. And the way to achieve that aim is for the teacher to be concerned about the child as an individual flame, to make our best effort to look into the child, to comprehend what this unique personality needs to become all that he or she can be.

I once knew a woman who was a Hebrew teacher, specializing in private tutoring for the mentally retarded and developmentally disabled. She gained something of a reputation, and parents from many miles around brought children to her to learn *brachos*, *aleph beis* and *bar-mitzvah* lessons.

She did all this in her home — this was in the 1950's, before the days of specialized texts and audio-visual aids — and it was a special source of pride for her when a child, whose parents had been told would never be able to read English, learned from her how to read Hebrew. The highpoint of her career was when a special-education center offered her a job which paid double what her husband was making — an offer which was later withdrawn when the center learned to their astonishment that this woman had no college degree and no professional training whatsoever.

She lacked all formal credentials and all the qualifications that might be inscribed on a university diploma. But this woman had a caring heart which wanted to help each child, to connect with that child's special soul and need. It is not a natural talent granted only to a few. It is a pathway, open to everyone; the willingness to make the effort to climb the steps, to look into the student, and to remain there until the flame burns brightly; and, with Hashem's help, those people intuitively find the way to the hearts of children and to the hearts of everyone whose lives they touch.

Shelach: Idealistic Temptations

The *sidrah* tells the story of the *meraglim*, the spies who visited *Eretz Yisrael* and who sinned by discouraging our ancestors from going there, thereby causing them to remain in the wilderness forty years. Before the spies departed, Moshe Rabbeinu changed the name of one of them, his disciple Hoshea Bin Nun, to Yehoshua. The name change was a form of prayer, just as we sometimes add a new name to a sick person as a kind of *tefillah*, and Moshe *davened* that Yehoshua should not fall into the trap of sinning by viewing *Eretz Yisrael* in an unfavorable light.

Why did Moshe pray for Yehoshua more than for others? Surely, he was not playing favorites. Was Yehoshua more liable to sin than the rest?

In making moral choices, sometimes we must choose between what is right and what is easy or pleasurable. Difficult as it may be to overcome desire or laziness, at least we usually know inside what the correct choice *should* be.

However, there exists another kind of temptation, where an unconscious desire is driving us to do the wrong thing, and in our conscious minds we rationalize to ourselves that the wrong choice is really the correct one. Since the temptation is not recognized for what it is, it is much more difficult to overcome.

The spies were princes of Israel, chosen for wisdom and good character to lead the people through the desert. They did not travel to *Eretz Yisrael* with clear intent to do wrong. But commentaries explain that in the wilderness these princes were leaders of the nation; once the Jews entered and divided *Eretz Yisrael*, the princes would be out of a job, no longer holding positions of power and prestige.

The realization that *Eretz Yisrael* meant a loss of their personal authority became what is known as a *shochad*, a bribe, an unconscious motivation causing them to view *Eretz Yisrael* through dark glasses, to decide the country was not good for Jews after all. The bribe of *kavod*, the desire for status and power, was a powerful temptation, especially when they were not aware of its existence on a conscious level.

However, as difficult as the temptation was for the spies, for Yehoshua it was much worse. Yehoshua was Moshe Rabbeinu's devoted disciple, and he had already heard the prophesy that Moshe would die before the nation entered *Eretz Yisrael*. The longer they remained outside the Land, the longer Yehoshua's beloved teacher would remain alive. What greater temptation was there to lie about the Land than to keep Moshe Rabbeinu alive and well? Since Yehoshua's temptation was greatest, Moshe *davened* for him in particular that his love for Moshe should not cause him to reach the wrong conclusion about *Eretz Yisrael*.

Shelach: Idealistic Temptations

This is a lesson for all of us; Whenever we are faced with decision-making, particularly when it concerns other people, we should be aware of the possibility that unconscious desires may be pushing us towards improper choices, and we must try to bring those desires out into the open. And we must be aware that if indeed the urge is an altruistic one, if our desire to speak against someone or do someone harm is motivated by our feeling for a *mitzvah*, then in that case — when there is no recognizable temptation, and no feeling of guilt to restrain us — we, like Yehoshua, must be doubly on guard not to fool ourselves, and not to end up lost in the desert, when we could be on our way to enjoying the blessings of *Eretz Yisrael*.

Korach: "It's the Principle of the Thing"

This *sidrah* tells the story of one of history's great acts of insanity, the rebellion of Korach. After witnessing all of Moshe Rabbeinu's miracles, including the Revelation at Mount Sinai, Korach still managed to delude himself into believing that he could overthrow Moshe, and that Hashem would grant him success. Our Sages say that, in general, Korach was a *pike'ach*, a perceptive man, and he possessed some measure of *ruach haKodesh*. How could someone so wise be so dense? How could he have such a wicked stupidity, which caused the death of himself and all his followers?

Rashi quotes the famous Midrash that the ultimate cause of Korach's downfall was envy. Initially, he had nothing against Moshe, but Korach had a cousin named Elitzafan, who is not even mentioned in the story of the rebellion in *Chumash.* When Moshe appointed Elitzafan to a position Korach had desired for himself, the Midrash says it was then that Korach exploded: "You're giving him the honor? It should be mine!"

Korach was much too refined to say this openly, probably too refined to even admit it to himself. Instead, he succeeded in persuading himself that Moshe had become arrogant and power-hungry. From there, Korach went on to develop a complete new ideology, a theory of sacred anarchy: since all Jews are holy, we don't need Moshe or any leader. He went so far as to reject certain *mitzvos,* asserting that a house containing a *Sefer Torah* should not require *mezuzos* on its doors, so as not to make any one parchment of Torah superior to others. He invented a religion and a dispute which endangered the entire nation, all because he did not receive the office he desired.

The Torah does not tell this story in order to speak *lashon hara* about Korach. Its purpose is to teach us to recognize, and to deal with, the Korachs in our lives today. We all know people who are quarrelsome, complaining, or difficult to live with in one way or another. The Torah is showing us: Whatever the other person is *kvetching* about may not be the problem which truly disturbs him. And therefore, even giving him what he asks for will not help matters, if that is not what he truly wants.

We must learn from Moshe Rabbeinu to try to respond to the other person's emotion, and not only to their statement. When Korach complained that everyone should be equal, Moshe said that Korach already had so much, why the need for more? That did not answer Korach's argument. But Moshe understood Korach's mind, and he gave the only reply that might possibly help. Even then, Korach refused to listen; but his children did, and they were saved.

The truly frightening aspect of this incident is: If envy could make Korach believe that Moshe was wicked, and if emotional turmoil led him to invent ridiculous theories out of thin air, then couldn't the same thing happen to you and me? Korach had a brilliant mind. If he could make such horrible mistakes, then perhaps our daily complaints and accusations are also false. Perhaps our views of reality are also distorted, and we are living in a state of permanent mental illness. Thoughtful people do not leave this *sidrah* cheering the destruction of villains. They are too busy wondering what would happen to themselves if miraculous earthquakes occurred tomorrow morning.

The all-important question becomes: When I am upset or angry with another person, how can I tell when I am fooling myself and twisting reality? If we could have that knowledge and apply it, it could radically change our lives (not to mention a good many marriages) for the better. I do not have *the* answer. But as a partial answer, try this suggestion on for size: As a rule of thumb, if someone thinks they are upset over "the principle of the thing," then they should be aware that they have become prisoners of Korachite delusion.

Reuven was cheated by an auto mechanic, and he burns with rage at the injustice of such wickedness in the world. But just last month, when Reuven heard that Shimon was cheated by a repair man, Reuven accepted that injustice with philosophic tranquility. The *yeshivah* dinner chairman publicly thanked the entire dinner committee by name, but he neglected to mention Mrs. Honeyfunkelmeyer, and she is furious: "That ingrate, such a lack of gratitude and *derech eretz!*" But last year, when Mrs. Levy's name was inadvertently omitted, Mrs. Honeyfunkelmeyer was the very soul of understanding: "People forget, it was unintentional," etc.

We are not disturbed by the evil that men do, only by the evil that men do to *us*. It is natural to feel hurt, and it is all right to admit that "I am sensitive, or over-sensitive, and I feel badly that I did not get what I wanted from the chairman or the *gabbai* or my spouse." But if we refuse to admit our weakness even to ourselves, if instead we become righteously indignant over the injustice of another person's wrongdoing; then even if wrong was truly done, the indignation invariably does not stem from righteousness. Once we allow a bruised ego to become a matter of principle, it is inevitable that we will lose touch with the reality of the situation, and fall victim to Korach's disease.

Our Sages say that in the instant when the earth opened up to swallow Korach's followers, Korach's own sons repented, and were saved. At that moment, the sons attained such holiness that they said *shirah*, a prophetic song of thanks to Hashem. Sometimes, the shock of falling is itself the inspiration to rise anew. And that realization can help clear the cobwebs of insanity from our minds, enabling us to see the true beauty of people all around us; and to sing songs of thanks for the blessings of life and friends and family, and of having other people around to receive the love we have to share.

Matos: Gratitude

In this *sidrah,* Hashem commands Moshe Rabbeinu to attack the nation of Midian, in retribution for Midian's attempt to destroy Israel as related in *Parashas Balak.* To fulfill the command, Moshe sent Pinchas to take charge, and did not himself go to battle. Rabbeinu Bachai explains why: "Moshe, who had lived in Midian, and who found his wife there at the well, did not go himself. As the saying goes: If you drank from a well, don't throw dirt into it." Although it was a *mitzvah* from Hashem to wage war against Midian, it was not a *mitzvah* for Moshe Rabbeinu to participate in person; because Moshe had an obligation to show gratitude to Midian for having lived there, and for benefits received.

We do not find that the people of Midian were particularly hospitable to Moshe. On the contrary, he had to fight Midianite shepherds to obtain water for the daughters of Yisro. The Midrash says that Yisro and his children, including Moshe's wife, were excommunicated by Midian because they did not worship idols. To top it all off, Midian now tries to wipe us out. And yet, Moshe is expected to demonstrate personal gratitude? That is like telling a Jew who escaped Soviet Russia, or for that matter Nazi Germany, that he should feel grateful to the country where he was born!

But it appears that the principle is: Gratitude is so important, that even if the benefactor treats us as an enemy, and the time comes when it is a *mitzvah* to fight him; nevertheless, even the necessity to go to war should not make us forget any benefits previously received.

In this *parashah* the Torah does not explain *why* this is so important, but our Sages told us: "Whoever denies (or forgets) a kindness received from other people, will also deny kindness received from *HaKadosh Baruch Hu.*" To relate to Hashem, we must be aware of the many blessings He gives us daily. But there is always something in life not to our liking, and someone who allows the complaint to push aside gratitude for goodness received will always find something to complain about. This is true in dealing with others, and true in dealing with the Creator; and such people will never be able to appreciate their blessings, or to enjoy them.

There are so many blessings we take for granted, so many roses which would give us pleasure if we would only stop talking about the thorns. To mention one small example so often overlooked: the blessings of children. When you hear parents complain about the hardship of child-rearing, ask them if they would consider giving up their child for adoption. If they are not grateful for that boy or girl, there are many thousands of childless couples on waiting lists who would be.

But the blessing of children is not only in children of your own, but also to enjoy the children of others. It was not so long ago that American Orthodox Judaism was viewed as a collective *moshav zekeinim*, a home for the immigrant generation and the aged. It might last another few decades, but by the 1960's or 70's, Torah observance would surely be extinct. A book published in 1929 entitled "Why I am a Jew" wondered whether, by 1970, there would even be a Jewish people at all.

How did the older people feel, seeing themselves as the last generation, believing that their synagogue and their *Yiddishkeit* would die with them? What was the pain of watching Hebrew-school children in *shul*, knowing that after *bar mitzvah* they would not be seen again?

But the Creator has a plan, and thanks to Him everything has changed. With tens of thousands of *mitzvah*-observant children in *shuls* and *yeshivos*, with Torah learning and *mitzvah* dedication going from strength to strength, the entire atmosphere has been transformed. When we see Jewish children in *shul* — even the children who come and run in the aisle, or who scream, cry, or drop candy wrappers — we must express to Hashem an enormous debt of gratitude for giving *them* — the Jewish future — to *us* and *Klal Yisrael*.

It is such a *simchah* that we *have* a future, that we hope to survive and grow, and that we can be more optimistic than even Jews in Eastern Europe were ninety years ago; it should make us want to say a warm "Good Shabbos" to every Jewish child, and to give them all as much candy as their mothers allow them to have.

What about the disturbances? The noise children make, the sticky lollipop you discover on your seat in the *Beis HaMidrash?* True, there are indeed a number of petty annoyances; especially in *shul*, we can always use a bit more decorum, and *mispallelim* should always encourage more reverence (beginning with the adults). But *chassidim* tell a story:

A wealthy man once complained to his *Rebbe*: "*Rebbe*, I happily give *tzedakah* to the poor. But when they walk into my parlor, and their boots track mud all over my expensive carpet, I just can't stand it!" The *Rebbe* replied with a story.

"There was once a wealthy man who gave *tzedakah* and performed many *mitzvos;* like most people, he also had his sins. While traveling on the road one day in his expensive carriage, he came across a poor peddler whose wagon had overturned, and who was trapped unconscious in the wreck. He ran over to help, and lay down in the mud to lift the broken wagon from the peddler's body. He carefully carried the unconscious victim to his own carriage, and brought him home to his mansion. The servants were startled to see their master covered in dirt, but the wealthy man had the peddler put to bed and cared for until he recovered, and then gave him enough money to buy another wagon to make a new start.

"Years passed, and the wealthy man died, and came before the Heavenly court for judgment. The defending angels brought in all the *mitzvos* he had to his credit; but since his life had been blessed with good fortune, more was expected of him, and the sins he had committed outweighed the *mitzvos* in the Divine scales of justice. Things were looking very bad indeed, when one of the angels brought the soul of the poor peddler and placed it on the scale. It was still not enough. The angel added to the scale the peddler's whole family, and the new wagon he had given them, and even the old wagon the wealthy man had lifted to save the peddler's life. It still wasn't enough to tip the scales.

"But just as the verdict was to be given, the defending angel said, 'Wait!' And he brought in heaps of mud, all the mud the wealthy man had rolled in to lift the wagon off the peddler, and all the mud from the peddler's clothes which had dirtied up the rich man's home. And the *zechus*, the *mitzvah* merit of that mud, tipped the scales to righteousness."

And the Rebbe turned to his own wealthy man: "Your *mitzvos* are praiseworthy, and the *tzedakah* you give is to your eternal credit. But in the World of Truth, your greatest *zechus* will not be for charity alone; it will be for your forbearance, that you allow the poor to enter your home although their boots are muddy and they do not know enough to remove them. That is your merit, most of all."

I have no documentation of the records of the Heavenly court, to verify the truthfulness of that story. But as the saying goes, even if it isn't true, it ought to be. The Gemara tells us that many people who go to *shul* do not pray correctly (that is at least as true today as it was in the past); and yet the Gemara says that Heaven rewards them, not so much for the *davening* as for the effort and discomfort involved in *going* to *shul*. Putting up with a little discomfort to honor a *mitzvah* is sometimes the greatest *mitzvah* of all.

We need not deliberately encourage discomfort. Someday, perhaps, all children will learn to behave politely in public, just as perhaps someday all adults will learn to sit quietly during *krias haTorah* and the repetition of the *Shemoneh Esrei*. But until then, let us still be exceedingly grateful for the blessings Hashem gives us, including the blessing of all the children, and all the adults; feeling the pride of having these people, and having a future for our community, and an ever-brighter future for all of *Klal Yisrael*.

Ki Seitzei: Divine Messengers

When you build a new home, make a fence around your roof, that you shall not bring blood upon your house, for one who falls will fall from it (Deuteronomy 22:8). If a new home, or even an old one, has a flat roof suitable for walking or sun-bathing, we are obligated to construct a fence around it to protect people from the danger of falling off.

The Gemara says that the *mitzvah* to prevent accidents applies also to other potential hazards, that "you shall not bring blood upon your house." This means it is a *mitzvah* obligation to get rid of a dangerous dog or frayed electrical wiring or roller skates on the stairs. Picking up a dropped banana peel or drying a wet floor where pedestrians might slip are acts of true holiness.

But the *pasuk* ends, *for one* who falls *will fall from it.* Why the superfluous term? *Rashi* quotes our Sages: The victim is called *one who falls* because he was destined to fall in any case, if not from your roof then from somewhere else. Even so, let you not be the cause of his death; for Heaven brings about goodness through the agency of good people, and evil through the agency of those who deserve evil.

This is a general principle. Our lives are in the Hands of Hashem, and no one can harm us without His consent. If we lose a wallet to a pickpocket, the criminal is certainly responsible for his crime; but had he not been there, we would still have been destined to lose the money, one way or another.

The same is true of blessings. If you receive a gift, be grateful to the giver for his kindness, but you should also know that if this particular benefactor did not exist, Hashem would have helped you in a different way. Everything comes from Heaven, but "goodness is brought about through the agency of good people, and evil through the agency of those who deserve evil." The one who falls was destined to fall from somebody's roof, but make a fence so that it should not be from yours.

Realizing that human activity is only a fulfillment of the Divine Plan can help us sail through life much more smoothly. When another person causes us pain, our reaction of bitterness and self-pity is often worse than the original harm. But if we accept that Hashem is in charge and He knows what is best for me; and if my neighbor had not insulted me, Hashem would have found someone else to do the job; then, without excusing the other's actions, it becomes easier for us to accept the pain, and to bear it gracefully.

This idea can also help us accept our own actions and limitations. We may try to help another or to benefit our community, and sometimes we fail. But ultimate success and failure are not in our hands, nor can parents and teachers expect even their own children to always turn out the way they would like. Our *mitzvah* is but to try. However, with all this in mind we can ask: "If Hashem controls everything that occurs, and if I don't do the work, someone else will; then why should I ever feel a burden of responsibility to do anything? The *yeshivah* needs money? If I don't contribute, Hashem will arrange for someone else to help! My children don't have enough Torah education? Hashem has a plan for the world, let Him worry about it!" Why is this not true, and why are we personally responsible for family, community and *klal*?

When the people of Israel in the wilderness were attacked by poisonous serpents, Moshe Rabbeinu was commanded to fashion a three-dimensional serpent image out of copper, for reasons explained by the commentaries. That copper image remained with us for centuries, as a national monument. Eventually, under the influence of Canaanite paganism, some Jews began to relate to this image as an object of veneration, a form of forbidden idol-worship. Finally, the righteous King Chizkiah performed the *mitzvah* of destroying it.

The Gemara asks: Jews had begun worshiping this serpent decades before King Chizkiah, and in those earlier times there had been righteous kings like Asa and Yehoshafat who dedicated themselves to wiping out idolatry. Why didn't Asa and Yehoshafat destroy the image? The Gemara answers: The previous kings left something unfinished; they left over the serpent so that Chizkiah would have some accomplishment to call his own.

At first glance, it appears as if those righteous men said: "If we destroy every single idol, Chizkiah will have nothing left to accomplish; so let us leave him one idol to smash!" But in the interval, people worshiped that idol, and those *tzaddikim* would not have permitted it to remain any more than they would have allowed a time bomb to lie ticking in the street. But the meaning is:

Hashem chooses certain people as His messengers, to achieve certain goals. King David, for example, unified the Jewish nation. Perhaps someone else would have done it, but

Hashem chose David; and therefore, until David came along, the job for one reason or another did not get done. Hashem wanted Chizkiah to be the *tzaddik* who destroyed the serpent. Therefore, when Asa was smashing all the idols years before, Hashem arranged that Asa overlooked this one for he did not realize that the national monument had become a danger. Asa did not consciously neglect the job; but when Heaven wants a particular person to do it, the job waits for him.

Today, when there are so many different Torah needs in our families and in our community, Hashem is still in complete charge, and the success of any project or institution is only up to Him. But each of us is put on earth with our own particular missions to fulfill, and when something needs doing, we must consider: Perhaps the Creator is waiting for His chosen messenger to do this job, and perhaps that messenger is *me*! Heaven certainly needs you for something, or else you wouldn't be here. And it is up to us to seek our opportunities to serve, until we discover that special something, the particular *mitzvah* or *mitzvos* which have been lying in wait for us all these years.

So the next time you sweep up broken glass, or change the battery in your fire alarm, or shovel snow to keep others from slipping on the sidewalk, remind yourself: Besides being a *mitzvah*, besides an act of sanctity, this also symbolizes a desire, a prayer that we should never become an agent of Divine tragedy, that the one who falls should never fall in our home. And it is also a reminder that we should be on the lookout for *mitzvah* opportunities which others may have neglected, to apply for the job of Hashem's messenger with humility, acknowledging that all success is up to Him; but with the pride of knowing that "Heaven brings about goodness through the agency of those who are good."

Ki Savo:
Mitzvah Blessings

To speak of one's own success, anything that smacks of boasting, is considered vulgar, if not downright sinful. But in this *sidrah* we find at least one occasion when it is a *mitzvah* to publicize personal achievement, in the commandment of *viddui ma'aser*.

The farmer in *Eretz Yisrael* is commanded to separate a number of tithes, portions of his crop for *Kohanim*, *Leviim* and the poor. If he observed all the *halachos* correctly for three years, he is invited to the *Beis HaMikdash* for a "victory celebration" on the last day of Pesach, when thousands of righteous farmers would assemble to declare: "We did it! We fulfilled our *mitzvos*. Hashem, please continue to give us your blessings." It was an exciting event, and a great honor to be part of it.

Included in the farmer's declaration was *I did not transgress Your commands and I did not forget* (Deuteronomy 26:13). The Midrash notes that forgetting a commandment is also a form of transgression; if the farmer could say that he did not transgress, why must he add that he did not forget? The Midrash answers: "Transgressing" refers to the act of taking the tithe; "forgetting" refers to the *brachah*, the blessing recited on taking the tithe. *I did not forget* means that when the farmer separated *terumah* or *ma'aser* or *challah*, he did not forget to say the *brachah* that accompanies the *mitzvah*. If he *did* forget, he is not entitled to make the declaration and be part of the winner's circle in *Yerushalayim*.

But there is a problem here. It is a general principle of *halachah* that performing a *mitzvah* without saying the required *brachah* does not affect fulfillment of the *mitzvah* itself. One who puts on *tefillin* or shakes a *lulav* but omits the *brachah* thereby loses the Rabbinic *mitzvah* to recite the *brachah*, but the Biblical *mitzvah* of *tefillin* or *lulav* is nonetheless complete. Why then does the Torah say that if the farmer omitted the *brachah* for tithing, it affects the *mitzvah* itself and invalidates his declaration?

There is a parallel to this in the *halachos* of *shechitah*, kosher slaughter. According to one opinion, if a *shochet* slaughtered a cow without first saying the *brachah* on the mitzvah of *shechitah*, the cow is not kosher! That opinion is not accepted by most authorities, but even minority views must be based on some Torah principle. What reason is there to void a *mitzvah* merely because its *brachah* is missing?

Rav Yaakov Kamenetzky z.l. answered: The essence of many *mitzvos* is a positive act, like shaking a *lulav*, eating *matzah*, hearing the *shofar*, etc. Other *mitzvos* are not so much positive acts as they are the removal of a negative; salting meat to remove blood, for example, is not so much a positive *mitzvah*-act as it is a necessary step to remove the non-kosher status of the food. This explains why there is no *brachah* recited before salting meat, since the salting is not in itself the *mitzvah*.

Some *mitzvos* are positive, others are a removal of a negative, and some *mitzvos* are both. The *terumah* tithe, for instance, is a positive *mitzvah*-act to express gratitude to Hashem by separating a percentage of the crop to give to a *Kohen*. In addition, there is a negative aspect, that the food is forbidden to eat until the tithe has been taken. In performing this *mitzvah* the farmer should therefore have two *kavanos*, two objectives in mind: taking the tithe to remove the prohibition from the food, and also the positive *mitzvah*-act to demonstrate thanks to the Creator.

But what if a farmer doesn't care about gratitude to Hashem, what if he has no interest in the positive aspect of the *mitzvah*? What if his only reason for tithing is to make the crop permitted by removing the prohibition against untithed food? In that case, Rav Yaakov pointed out, such a farmer would separate the tithe but would most likely *not* recite the *brachah*. In his mind, he is only removing a negative, like salting meat, and there is no *brachah* for that.

And in such cases the Torah says: True, you fulfilled your basic *mitzvah* obligation. But you are not eligible to enter the winner's circle, you cannot join the champions in *Yerushalayim*. You are not a sinner. But if you forgot the *brachah*; if you did not feel the *mitzvah* was something positive; if you did not feel that in giving the tithe you were getting something in return; then the victory celebration is not yours for you won't be able to grasp what the *simchah* is all about.

This also explains the *mitzvah* of *shechitah*. An animal which died of any cause other than via the *shechitah* method may not be eaten, and *shechitah* is necessary to remove the standing prohibition. But besides removing a negative, *shechitah* is also a positive act symbolizing that our food is tied to our loyalty to Hashem, and that eating can be holy; and the *shochet* therefore recites a *brachah*. One who omits the *brachah* demonstrates (according to one opinion) that he sees no sanctity in his eating, it is not service to Hashem, he desires only to remove the *treifah* status from his cow — in such cases, it is better not to eat meat at all.

There is a lesson here for all of us. Some people perform a *mitzvah* merely to be free of the obligation. Others perform the same *mitzvah*, but with an attitude of trying to get all the positive benefit from it, the *brachah*, the blessing of the *mitzvah*. It is only that second type of Jew who will be able to proclaim his pride in what he does, his feelings of achievement and victory.

If a family keeps the Shabbos, but shares no words of Torah at the Shabbos table, no singing, and no learning on Shabbos afternoon, can they expect to feel the full joy of what Shabbos is? If we *daven*, but approach *davening* as an exercise in speed-reading, or as something to do in intervals between conversations with the fellow in the next row, can we ever hope to experience the awesome elevation of prayer?

The same is true in human relations. A well-mannered young man who was having marital problems told me: "I cannot understand why my wife is so upset. I fulfill all the obligations of a Jewish husband, whatever it says in the *sefarim*, in the books." I grabbed him gently by the neck and replied, "Dear *shoiteh* (fool), do you think marriage is a list of obligations to check off? That if you smile twice a day, and mechanically say 'I love you' at regular intervals, that is called building a relationship?" If there is no positive effort to feel for the other person and to share *with* that person, can we expect to have any kind of meaningful future five or ten years down the road?

We need not be philosophers, and we need not understand all the secret meanings of each *mitzvah*. But if we can only remember that every *brachah* is a way of saying, "*Lechaim,*" that the *mitzvah* is indeed something to celebrate; a positive experience adding something to my life, my *Yiddishkeit*, and my idealism; then by trying our best to savor the *mitzvah* we will also be worthy to enter the winner's circle, celebrating the blessings of being who we are, and asking Hashem to increase those blessings, every day of the year.

Ki Savo: Mitzvah Blessings

Nitzavim: Covenant

Before Moshe Rabbeinu passed away, he assembled Israel *to bring you into the covenant of Hashem your God and His oath* (*Deuteronomy* 29:11). We already had the covenant made with Avraham and the covenant of Mount Sinai. What is this additional covenant, which the Torah says is for all generations? Moshe also warned those who might reject the covenant: *Hashem will not be willing to forgive* (*ibid*. 29:19), strong words for a contractual agreement which most of us know virtually nothing about.

Interestingly, *Parashas Nitzavim* also contains the *mitzvah* of *teshuvah*, that we can make amends for sin and be forgiven (*ibid*. 30:10). This appears only a few lines after Moshe tells us that Hashem will not forgive. Does He or doesn't He?

The *Chasam Sofer* explains that there is a difference between a normal contract and a *bris*, a covenant. A contract is in effect only if all its stipulations are carried out; if one party does not fulfill his obligations, the other party is freed from any reciprocal obligation in return. But a *bris*, a covenant, *binds* the two parties. Even if one of them is negligent or worse, the bond remains.

Marriage is a covenant. Supper may be burnt, the trash may not have been taken out, a hundred transgressions large and small can be endured if the relationship itself is understood to be binding to begin with. But even in a covenantal agreement, if one partner denies the covenant itself, e.g. if the husband leaves his wife for another, then the relationship is gone, and the bond is broken.

In *Parashas Nitzavim,* Hashem swore an oath to our fathers, that we are His people and *Eretz Yisrael* is our land. We in turn swore loyalty to the Torah and its *mitzvos.* But "there is no *tzaddik* on earth who does only good without ever a sin." If we fail to keep our promise, what ensures that Hashem will keep His?

But the *parashah* also contains the *mitzvah* of *teshuvah*, and the *Chasam Sofer* offers a radically new insight: Since repentance is a *mitzvah,* then sinning is somehow *also* included in the Torah, transgression is also covered by the relationship. We must do our best not to err; but with all our errors, the bond between us and Hashem remains intact.

The covenant of *Nitzavim* is that we remain Hashem's people with all our failings. Sin demands *teshuvah*, and going against the Torah causes self-inflicted harm leading to retribution, but the Divine relationship continues without a break. And, the *Chasam Sofer* explains, the only way we can lose the benefit of this eternal covenant is if we ourselves refuse to acknowledge that the covenant still exists.

A Jew who is weak or lustful, but who admits his shortcomings, is still part of the *bris*; and the *mitzvah* of *teshuvah* awaits him, today or tomorrow. But, as it says in the *parashah*, *If, when he hears the words of the oath, he blesses himself in his heart and says, I will have peace* — I am quite satisfied with what I am — *and I will walk according to the whim of my desires* (*ibid.* 29:18); if someone asserts that he doesn't *need* the *mitzvos,* and he thereby severs himself from the covenant, then *Hashem will not be willing to forgive* (*ibid.* v. 19), because the relationship no longer exists.

Perhaps this is why the *mitzvah* of *bris milah* and the prohibition against intermarriage have always been so dear to us. A Jewish male without *bris milah* transgresses the Torah, but no more so than one who eats *cheilev*, forbidden animal fats. When a Jew marries a gentile, the tragedy of the halachic violation is technically not worse than that of a Jewish couple who violate the *halachos* of family purity. And yet, until very recently, even non-observant Jews knew: A Jewish baby boy must have a *bris*, and intermarriage is where we draw the line, because these are *mitzvos* of the *covenant*, and whatever else we observe or transgress, to shatter the covenant is to rip ourselves away from the eternity that is *Klal Yisrael.*

It was customary at one time for rabbis to preach only twice a year, *Shabbos HaGadol* before Pesach and *Shabbos Shuvah* before Yom Kippur. The *Chasam Sofer* suggests that the origin of the *Shabbos Shuvah drashah* is a midrash which says: "When the Sage teaches Torah to the public, the Almighty forgives the sins of Israel." Why is a *drashah* in *public* more conducive to forgiveness? Perhaps the answer is that even for those who fall asleep during the sermon, the mere fact that everyone assembles to hear it is a public demonstration: Whatever sins we commit, we come together to renew the covenant as a people loyal to Hashem; and the eternal bond remains.

Similarly, the *Chasam Sofer* explains why one of the Ten Commandments is not to swear falsely, and why one who would make a false oath is so strongly condemned. It is because a person who swears to an untruth is someone who does not know the meaning of a sacred commitment, *any* commitment. Such a person cannot enter into a covenant for he has lost the ability to bind himself into a relationship and to create permanence in whatever good he may do.

In human relations, modern freedoms seem to have weakened our sense of personal responsibility in general, and many people find it difficult to make long-term commitments to marriage or to anything else. Having lost any sense of belonging to the covenant, individuals end up feeling that they belong to nothing at all, and freedom becomes the cruel joke of being free to choose between one meaningless whim and another.

So in a real sense, part of preparing for Yom Kippur is not only to strive to become a *tzaddik*, but to first learn to be a sinner; one who admits that "yes, I have been lax, and I am indeed guilty of such and such." We should admit to Hashem and to ourselves that the covenant means everything to us, so much so that we are willing to openly confess our wrongdoing to Him, and to request His aid to return.

Also, since the basis of a covenant is the sanctity of oaths, for which reason the Torah so strongly condemns a false oath, the Days of Repentance are also a time to be extra careful to honor any kind of commitment made, even without an actual oath. Any sort of pledge should be followed up quickly, appointments kept punctually, and in every agreement our word should be a sacred bond. This will help strengthen our feelings for commitment in general, to give us the power to make real commitments to all that is truly important; to renew the covenant, and to be worthy of *Nitzavim's* promise of Hashem's love and His redemption, on *Yamim Noraim* and all through the year.

Ha'azinu: Seventy Nations

Hashem established the boundaries of nations according to the number of the Children of Israel (*Deuteronomy* 32:8). This means that national boundaries, the distinctions between different national entities, are somehow linked to the *number* of the Children of Israel. *Rashi* writes, "for the sake of the seventy members of the Children of Israel who went down to Egypt, He established the boundaries of the nations as seventy languages." This requires some explanation.

Our tradition is that when the world was young, the Creator arranged for the development of seventy different nations. We think of "nations" as peoples who inhabit particular political states; but the Torah concept is of a particular kind of people with a distinct national character, what we might call a culture. The differences between Frenchmen, Arabs and Japanese are much more than geography and government. There are distinct differences in thinking, modes of expression and action.

Over the centuries, nations have intermarried and intermingled so that the distinctions are not as clear cut as they once were. But it appears from the Gemara that each of the original seventy peoples had its own spiritual character, with its own angel in Heaven to represent it. Even today, those seventy forms of character, seventy ways to look at life, still exist, scattered among the nations of the world. But why did Hashem create seventy nations, and not sixty or eighty? They were created *according to the number of the Children of Israel,* to correspond to our seventy ancestors who made up the original Jewish nation in Egypt.

The *Ramban* explains that the Sanhedrin has seventy judges, and seventy family members created the Jewish people, because seventy is the number of individuals required to be able to include all the different points of view, and all the different spiritual powers. To try to understand this on a simple level, there are basically seventy different aspects through which honest, intelligent, learned people view the world. Truth is one, but from various vantage points we perceive varied facets of that truth. For this reason we did not become a nation until we were seventy; and the Sanhedrin must also have seventy, to enable the Torah nation to see the Torah and the universe with the most complete view.

But *Parashas Ha'azinu* adds the information that the seventy nations, seventy kinds of cultural perspective, are also meant to correspond to the seventy ways of thinking in Israel. This means: Each nation is meant to contribute some good to the world, and to contribute in its own way to the Jewish people. *Rav Tzadok of Lublin* wrote that the prophets lamented the destruction of pagan nations, even our enemies, because even in their destruction there is some spiritual loss for all of us.

We do not have a tradition to explain what each nation's particular contribution is meant to be (although the Gemara gives a few insights, e.g. "Rabbi Akiva said, In three things I love the Medes: They cut meat only on the table, they kiss only on the hand, and they take counsel only in the field" — *Brachos* 8b), and in any case, the original national groups no longer exist. Even so, we can speculate:

In the field of *kashrus* supervision, American rabbis of German background have long enjoyed a reputation of being exceptionally honest, meticulous and efficient. In general, German Jews are known for honesty, punctuality and a sense of order, and their New York *Kehillah* is probably the only non-chassidic group in the country with such a cohesive sense of communal structure. It is striking that a large percentage of *yeshivah mashgichim*, who lecture on what might be called "Torah ethics and philosophy," are also of German background.

Is it a coincidence that German *gentiles* are also known for neatness, efficiency, a sense of order and philosophy? Surely, we have here a case of non-Jewish influence on Jews, for good. Germany is not a righteous nation, and its history shows it to be the very opposite. But even Germans, even *their* cultural heritage has some good in it, which contributes to the spiritual mission of *Klal Yisrael*.

In Torah learning, no *yeshivah* today can equal the *yeshivos* of pre-war Eastern Europe. But Europeans themselves have noted that the atmosphere in American *yeshivos* is generally more friendly than it was in old *yeshivos*. The spirit of egalitarian camaraderie, the relative ease with which newcomers make friends in our *yeshivos* is not because Americans work harder at the *mitzvah* of Love Your Neighbor; but because the spirit of America is that way, an atmosphere of informal equality which has its drawbacks, but also has added something for our good.

The level of Torah observance in England is about the same as that of the United States, but a much higher percentage of non-observant Jews belong to Orthodox synagogues in England; because the English Jew, like the English gentile, has great respect for tradition. Just as his grandfather was not *shomer Shabbos* but attended an Orthodox *shul,* he too, is not *shomer Shabbos*, but the *shul* he attends (or does not attend) is Orthodox.

The Chinese are known for their reverence for old age. The Japanese have their appreciation of understated beauty, and the knowledge that eating is intimately tied to ritual, as in the Tea Ceremony. The dances of India, which are pagan, recognize the significance of symbolic gesture — an Indian Jew has a special feeling for what it means to shake a *lulav.* It was African-Americans' militancy in the 1960's which popularized the idea of ethnic pride and daring to be different, and Jews who today proudly wear *yarmulkes* in public must thank those who wore dashikis and Afro-hairdos back then.

We certainly do not need to copy non-Jews, and we must always remain on guard against negative influences of the society around us. But sadly, because of all our centuries of wandering, we no longer know what many of the original authentic Jewish characteristics were. When modern settlement of *Eretz Yisrael* began, questions of defining Jewish "character" and "culture" were hotly debated. Regrettably, the mass of Jews did not turn to the Torah for answers. Even more regrettably, the contemporary Torah community has still not clearly articulated its answers to offer the masses an attractive alternative today.

For instance, why do some non-observant Jewish caterers think that "Orthodox" and "ostentatious" are synonyms? We cringe to hear Jewish women referred to as "J.A.P.S," but the best way to counter a negative stereotype is to create a positive image to take its place.

The Yom Kippur service makes mention of Noach and his children, to pray for the welfare of all peoples; and on Succos, seventy offerings were brought in the *Beis HaMikdash* on behalf of the seventy nations. The reading of *Parashas Ha'azinu* at this time of year is therefore an opportunity to again consider *boundaries of nations*; what good qualities each one adds to the world, and what are the negative qualities for us to reject. By viewing the world correctly, and using it to accomplish our own unique mission, we bring closer the day of joy for everyone; when all the nations will come to *Yerushalayim* to celebrate Succos together with us, and to learn from us the wisdom of Hashem.

Glossary

aleph beis — (a) Hebrew alphabet; (b) in the context of this book — the basic foundation of a specific premise

aliyah [pl. **aliyos**] — (a) the act of being called to participate in the congregational Torah reading; (b) the individual portion read by the reader

Aron Kodesh — Holy Ark

Aseres HaDibros — Ten Commandments

aveirah — sin

Avinu — our father

avodah zarah — idolatry

ba'al teshuvah — a penitent; colloquially: an individual who, having led a secular life-style, adopts Orthodoxy

beis hak'nesses — synagogue

Beis HaMidrash — study hall

Beis HaMikdash — Holy Temple in Jerusalem

beneshikah — with a Divine kiss

bimah — lectern

Bircas Hamazon — Grace after Meals

bitachon — trust in G-d

brachah [pl. **brachos**] — blessing

bris — covenant

bris milah — circumcision performed according to *halachah*

b'tzelem Elokim — in the Divine image

chacham [pl. **chachamim**] — sage, scholar, wise person

chalilah — G-d forbid

challah — the *mitzvah* of removing a portion from bread dough in commemoration of the portion given to the *Kohen*

chametz — leaven, forbidden on Pesach

chas veshalom — G-d forbid

chassid [pl. **chassidim**] — (a) disciple of a chassidic Rebbe; (b) pious individual

chassidishe Rebbe — spiritual leader of a chassidic community

chatas — offering brought to atone for a transgression

Chazal — Torah Sages

cheder — Hebrew elementary school

cheilev — forbidden animal fats

chesed — kindness

chiddush [pl. **chiddushim**] — see **chiddushei Torah**

chiddushei Avodah — novel actions through which to serve G-d

chiddushei Torah — novel Torah insights

chinuch — education

chizuk — encouragement

chukim — commandments that have no apparent rational basis

Chumash [pl. **Chumashim**] — lit. a fifth. The Torah (Pentateuch) is comprised of five books, each called a *Chumash*. Often the entire Pentateuch is referred to as *Chumash*.

chumrah [pl. **chumros**] — stringency

chupah — (a) wedding ceremony; (b) the canopy under which the ceremony is held

chutzpah — nerve, gall

da'as — (a) full moral comprehension; (b) knowledge

daven — pray

davening — praying

degalim — flags

derech — lit. path, manner, approach

Derech Eretz — (a) work; (b) manner, politeness, decency

Devar Hashem — the Word of Hashem

devar Torah [pl. **divrei Torah**] — Torah exposition

drashah — speech

eish — fire

eishes chayil — woman of valor

eizer kenegdo — helpmate

Elul — the last month of the Jewish year

Eretz Yisrael — the Land of Israel

frumkeit — adherence to Orthodoxy

ga'avah — pride

gabbai — functionary who supervises the synagogue procedure

gadlus — greatness

gadol — Torah giant

gadol hador [pl. **gedolei hador**] — spiritual leader of the generation
gaon — brilliant Torah scholar
Gehinnom — perdition
Gemara — the part of the Talmud that expounds upon the Mishnah
geshmak — (Yiddish) enjoyable
gut vort — (Yiddish) bon mot; apt phrase
hachnasas orchim — hospitality to guests
Haggadah — story of the Exodus from Egypt which is related at the Pesach *Seder*
HaKadosh Baruch Hu — The Holy One, Blessed is He
hakaras hatov — (a) recognition of good; (b) the obligation to express gratitude to one's benefactor
halachah — [pl. **halachos**] — (a) a Torah law; (b) [cap.] the body of Torah law
Hallel — lit. praise; prayer on Pesach, Succos, Shavuos, Chanukah and Rosh Chodesh. It consists of Psalms 113-118.
hanhagah — custom
hashgachah pratis — Divine Providence
hashkafah — ideology
hatzlachah — success
hesped — eulogy
im yirtzeh Hashem — if Hashem wills
Imeinu — our mother
ish [pl. **anashim**] — man
ishah [pl. **nashim**] — woman
Kaddish — prayer recited at the daily services and other occasions by those who have lost a close relative
kallah — bride
kapparah — atonement for sin
kashrus — Jewish dietary law
kavanah [pl. **kavanos**] — objective in mind, intent concentration
kavod — honor, respect
kavod Shabbos — honor of the Sabbath
kavod Shamayim — (a) Divine glory; (b) honor of G-d
kedushah — holiness
Kehillah — (a) congregation; (b) community
keruvim — cherubim; two golden angels that were fashioned for the *Mishkan*
kibud av v'eim — honoring one's father and mother

Kiddush — prayer recited on the Sabbath and *Yom Tov* (usually over wine) in commemoration of the day
kiddush Hashem — sanctification of G-d's Name
klal — group, community
Klal Yisrael — Jewish people
kochos hanefesh — traits of fundamental personality
Kohen [pl. **kohanim**] — lit. priest, one of the priestly family descended from Aaron
Kohen Gadol — High Priest
kollel — higher academy of higher Jewish learning, whose students are married
korban [pl. **korbanos**] — sacrificial offerings
krias haTorah — the reading of the Torah in the synagogue
kvetch(ing) — (Yiddish) complain(ing)
lashon hara — lit. evil speech; disparaging statements (defamatory speech) made about another person
Lechaim — To life! The wish commonly made when people share a drink
lo lishmah — ulterior motive
lulav — palm branch — one of the Four Species which we are commanded to hold on the festival of Succos
Ma'ariv — the evening prayer service
ma'aser — tithe
machlokes — dispute
machzor — prayer book for the festivals
maris ayin — lit. appearance to the eye; an act which gives the *impression* of wrongdoing
mashal — analogy
mashgiach [pl. **mashgichim**] — (a) *kashrus* supervisor; (b) spiritual supervisor of Torah ethics in a *yeshivah*
Mashiach — Messiah
mazal — good fortune
mazal tov — lit. good luck

meilitz yosher — good petitioner; usually used in reference to the departed, that they should entreat G-d on behalf of the living

menorah — (a) candelabra; (b) the seven-branched candelabrum standing in the *Beis HaMikdash*; (c) the eight-branched candelabrum used on Chanukah

mentch — (Yiddish) decent person

mentchlichkeit — (Yiddish) decency

meraglim — spies

mes mitzvah — a dead body without anyone to bury it

meshuga — crazy

mesiras nefesh — unusual effort/devotion

metzora — one who is afflicted with *tzara'as* (a skin disease described in *Lev.* ch. 13)

mezuzah [pl. **mezuzos**] — a parchment scroll which contains the passages *Deut.* 6:4-9 and 11:13-21, and is affixed to the doorpost

middah [pl. **middos**] — character trait

Midrash — the body of Sages' teachings based on Scriptural verses

Mikdash — see Beis HaMikdash

mikdash m'at — miniature Sanctuary — used to connote synagogue or study hall

mikveh — ritualarium; a body of water which, by means of immersion, purifies people and objects from a state of *tumah* (ritual impurity)

milah — see *bris milah*

minhag [pl. **minhagim**] — custom

minyan — quorum of ten adult males necessary for certain prayers

mishega'as — (Yiddish) foolishness

Mishkan — Tabernacle, the portable Temple used by the Jews during their sojourn in the wilderness

mishpachah — family

mishpatim — Torah laws whose rationale is apparent

mispallelim — those who pray

mitzvah [pl. **mitzvos**] — (a) G-d's command; (b) good deed

mohel — one who performs ritual circumcisions

moser — informer

moshav zekeinim — old-age home

mussar — (a) rebuke; (b) ethical and religous teachings

nasi [pl. **nesiim**] — the leader of a tribe of Israel

navi — prophet

nechamah — consolation

nefesh — soul

nekamah — revenge

neshamah — soul

nisayon — challenge, test

nosei be'ol im chaveiro — sharing the burden of one's friend

Olam Haba — World to Come

oneg Shabbos — (a) a social gathering convened to celebrate the Sabbath with song, refreshment and Torah discussion; (b) the *mitzvah* of engaging in pleasurable pursuits on the Sabbath

parashah — weekly portion of the Torah

pashut — obvious, self-evident

pasuk — a verse of Scripture

Pesach — Passover

pike'ach — wise and perceptive individual

Rabbeinu — our teacher

rasha [pl. **reshaim**] — wicked individual

rebbe — teacher; chassidic leader

Ribono Shel Olam — Master of the Universe

Rishonim — medieval commentators on the Torah

rodef shalom — (1) to pursue peace; (2) a pursuer of peace

Rosh Chodesh — the first day of a month

ruach — spirit, enthusiasm

ruach haKodesh — Divine spirit or inspiration

Sanhedrin — high rabbinical court in Jerusalem

Satan — *yetzer hara*

Seder — (a) the series of rituals performed on the night of Passover; (b) set time

sefer [pl. **sefarim**] — (a) book; (b) Torah book

Sefer Torah [pl. **Sifrei Torah**] — Torah scroll

sefirah — lit. counting; (a) the period of 49 days between Pesach and Shavuos; (b) the *mitzvah* of counting the days of this period; also called *Sefiras HaOmer*
sha'atnez — (a) the prohibition against wearing an item of clothing which contains both linen and wool; (b) a forbidden blend of wool and linen
Shabbos — Sabbath
Shabbos HaGadol — the Sabbath before Passover
Shabbos Shuvah — the Sabbath between Rosh Hashanah and Yom Kippur
Shacharis — morning prayers
shalom — peace
Shamayim — Heaven
shammas — synagogue sexton
Shas — Talmud
Shavuos — Pentecost, Festival commemorating the giving of the Torah
Shechinah — Divine Presence
shechitah — kosher ritual slaughter
sheivet — tribe (of Israel)
Shemoneh Esrei — the main prayer of the daily prayer services
sheva brachos — (a) the seven blessings recited at weddings and the ensuing series of celebrations; (b) colloquially: the celebrations themselves
shidduch [pl. **shidduchim**] — matching of a man and woman for the purpose of marriage
shirah — song; in this instance, a (prophetic) song of praise and thanks to Hashem
shiur [pl. **shiurim**] — lecture on Torah subjects
shlishi — the third section of the Torah reading
shlita (שליט״א) — acronym of שֶׁיִּחְיֶה לְאוֹרֶךְ יָמִים טוֹבִים וְאֲרוּכִים, *may he live a long and good life*
shochad — a bribe
shochet — ritual slaughterer
Shomer Shabbos — one who observes the Sabbath
shoteh — fool
shtiebel — small synagogue
shtus [pl. **shtusim**] — foolishness

shul — synagogue
siddur — prayerbook
sidrah [pl. **sidros**] — weekly portion(s) of the Torah
simchah — (a) joy; (b) joyous occasion
sinah — hatred
sofer [pl. **sofrim**] — scribe
Succos — the Festival of Tabernacles
taharas hamishpachah — laws of family purity governing marital relations
talmid chacham [pl. **talmidei chachamim**] — Torah scholar
Tanach — the Written Torah, the Bible
tatte — (Yiddish) father
tefillah [pl. **tefillos**] — prayer
tefillin — phylacteries
Tehillim — Psalms
terumah — the first portion of the crop which must be separated and given to the *Kohen*
teshuvah — repentance
treifah — non-kosher
tza'ar [pl. **tzaros**] — pain, trouble
tza'ar gidul banim — the pain of raising children
tzaddik [pl. **tzaddikim**] — righteous person
tzara'as — an affliction of the skin (often mistakenly translated as leprosy)
tzedakah — charity
Yamim Noraim — High Holy Days (Rosh Hashanah and Yom Kippur)
yeshivah ketanah — see **cheder**
yetzer hara — evil inclination
yetzer hatov — inclination to do good
Yiddishkeit — Judaism
yirah — fear, reverence
yiras Shamayim — fear of Heaven
yisurim — suffering
Yom Kippur Kattan — the day before Rosh Chodesh is traditionally a day of repentance, a miniature Yom Kippur
Yom Tov [pl. **Yamim Tovim**] — Festival
yorei Shamayim — G-d-fearing individual
zaken [f. **zekeinah**; pl. **zekeinim**] — an elderly person
zayde — (Yiddish) grandfather
zechus — merit
zemiros — songs
zocheh — worthy

This volume is part of
THE ARTSCROLL SERIES®
an ongoing project of
translations, commentaries and expositions
on Scripture, Mishnah, Talmud, Halachah,
liturgy, history, the classic Rabbinic writings,
biographies, and thought.

For a brochure of current publications
visit your local Hebrew bookseller
or contact the publisher:

Mesorah Publications, ltd

4401 Second Avenue
Brooklyn, New York 11232
(718) 921-9000